P9-DUT-700

Needlepoint Design

Needlepoint Design

by LOUIS J. GARTNER Jr.

A House & Garden Book

William Morrow & Company, Inc. New York

Designed by James Craig

Library of Congress Catalog Card Number 70-121692

Printed and bound in the United States of America
by Quinn & Boden Company, Inc., Rahway, N.J.

Color work by Meulenhoff International, Amsterdam, Holland

4   5   75   74   73   72   71

Acknowledgments

My deepest thanks to the four M's, without whose constant encouragement, enthusiasm and criticism very little needlepoint shown in this book would ever have been finished . . .

. . . to Narcisse Chamberlain and Annett Francis for making the writing of the book possible . . .

. . . and to Kurt Miehlman, Bill Grigsby, Ernest Beadle and Ed Kasper for their photographs and illustrations.

Contents

List of Color Pictures

Needlepoint Design

Which Kind of Needlepointer Are You?

Few people have any idea how easy it is to design their own needlepoint with the modern materials and methods that are now available. Despite the excellent prepared needlepoint canvases we can buy today, all needlepointers get ideas of their own that would be much more rewarding to do if only they knew how to get them onto canvas themselves. It is a consideration, too, that prepared needlepoint canvases are very expensive. The ones you design yourself are not.

Extraordinarily popular as needlepoint has become recently, nevertheless almost nothing has been written about the simple mechanics of putting one's own designs on canvas nor about how to arrive at designs that suit each particular needlepointer. This book is all about how to do this, and must begin with a word about "which kind of needlepointer are you?"

From watching the many people I have taught to do needlepoint, I feel they fall very roughly into two categories. To begin with those who appear to be more "advanced," some needlepointers naturally tend to "paint" almost freehand with the wool colors on the canvas; they have a natural bent toward realism, shading, modeling, and quite probably could execute the same designs in several media — paint, pastel, pencil, or whatever. This is a talent that can be learned, but it is not the object of this book to teach drawing and painting! I only mean to show, if you have such skills, how they can be translated into the medium of needlepoint.

The other kind of needlepointer tends to do more forthrightly decorative designs, with colors and shapes laid on more flatly and with whatever intricacy there may be devoted more to color scheme and pattern than to realistic rendering. Anybody at all, the rankest beginner, can do this successfully. It is, even when quite elaborate, not so very different from filling in colors in a coloring book. This is the approach that is likely to apply to more "modern" or "abstract" designs and it can be used for designs as simple or as complicated as you want. Obviously, a simple decorative idea is the way to begin if you feel you have limited drawing and painting talent, but you can go on to fabulous designs still without ever bothering with "realism" in your needlepoint if it doesn't suit you.

I have been amused and pleased, though, to see people develop skills that they never knew they had for creating effects on canvas. Needlepoint is a deliberate, unhurried, soothing pastime. Little things begin to happen as you use the wool colors, experiments give unexpected results, and it just may be that the supposedly awesome process of shading and modeling will become your thing after all.

Detail from color picture 12

3. *Yorkshire asleep (page 75)*

But it certainly does not have to. For my part, I have always been interested in both ways of designing and working needlepoint — when I think about the distinction at all, for lots of designs can't really be categorized quite one way or the other. At any rate, many types of needlepoint design are represented in this book. Don't be misled by some of the more elaborate projects into thinking that it is written only for experts. The practical advice in it applies to any level of skill, and is needed by the hapless beginner most of all.

All writers about needlepoint have a missionary zeal. We want everybody to try it. Women are natural needlepointers. So are men when they try; it just seldom occurs to them to try. Yet, for centuries, in Europe the great needle-wielders have been men — tailors, tapestry makers, fashion designers. From antiquity to this day, some form of embroidery on textiles or rugs has been the work of men in the Far East, the Middle East, North Africa. European surgeons are reported to keep their fingers nimble with needlework, and English gentlemen for a couple of centuries have been given to passing the time with needlework that you can see both in British museums and in leather-chaired studies of today's stately, and suburban, homes.

To me, needle, wool, and canvas are much the same as hammer, nails, and lumber. The products are not even so different; each is something you have figured out and *made*. And it does appear that men are likely to approach needlework more as a serious project than some women do. The owners of a needlepoint shop told me that sixty per cent of their customers are men and added confidentially that most of the finished needlepoint men bring in for blocking is a lot better than what women bring in. True, that shop is in a city loaded with artists and designers, but the point is that this craft has something to offer to a lot more people than one might suppose — which I hope this book will show. I have tried many crafts and needlepoint to me is plainly the most appealing and relaxing of any, besides being the most portable and convenient, with nothing to set up and nothing to clean up before and after you set to work.

To tempt anyone who looks into this book to take fast action, as many illustrations as possible were planned so that you can crib designs directly from the printed page if you want to. This is a how-to and reference book meant to show many different kinds of needlepointers how to tackle projects according to their own skills — those who have never done any needlepoint at all, those designing their own for the first time, or experts, to whom I offer some suggestions and advice hard to come by elsewhere.

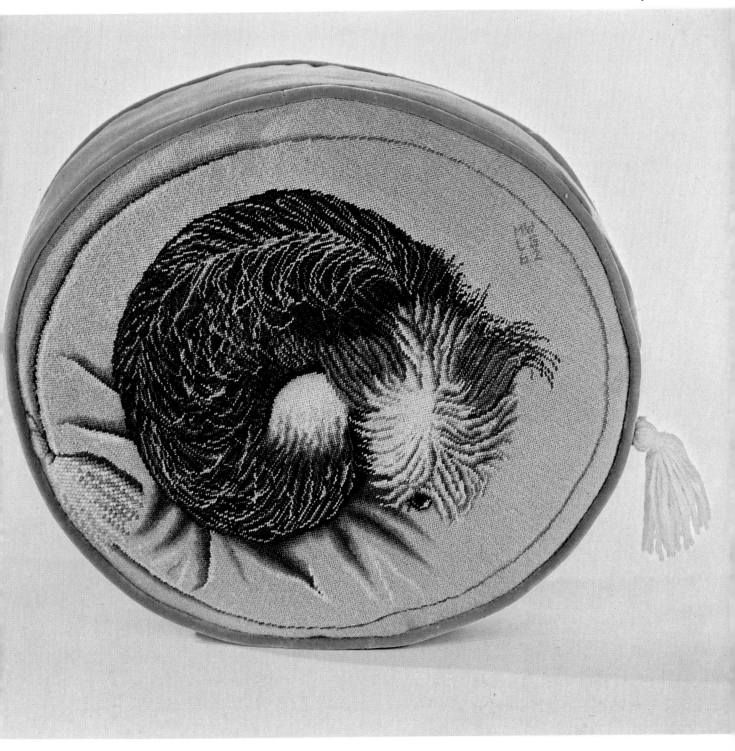

I have found that help of any kind on designing your own needlepoint is scarce indeed. The cost of having a professional put your ideas on canvas is likely to be exorbitant. Not only is it more than most of us can afford, it is also positively intimidating to work on a canvas that has cost you some enormous sum. Needlepoint should not be intimidating! It should be a rest and a pleasure, tailored to your own needs, not something you have to worry about. For these reasons, I think a book on needlepoint design is very much needed.

For beginners in particular, remember that the needlepoint stitch itself is one of the simplest in all needlecraft. Once you have mastered it, you can stop being concerned about how to do it and concentrate on achieving the right kind of design for you, one that you can't buy anywhere, an amusement all your own, and a lovely handmade thing that will be wonderfully satisfactory no matter how rudimentary you may think your first efforts should be. You will be surprised how difficult they *look*, even after you have discovered how easy they really are to do. And, someday, you will no doubt discover the needlepointer's almost fiendish delight in doing something absolutely as difficult as his imagination can think up. I hope you will find everything you need in this book to guide you from the first stage to the last.

L. J. G.

1 *The Tools of the Craft*

Needlepoint is a fabric, and a fabric that you invest with your own personality. A work of needlepoint begins, like an oil painting, as "canvas." The canvas of needlepoint is an open-mesh scrim, and there are varieties of scrim to accommodate projects large and small, ambitious and simple. The scrim is the canvas on which you "paint" with wool. Needle and yarn are your brush and paint. The comparison ends right there. Needlepoint parts company with actual painting because the color is applied with the repetition of a single basic stitch rather than with strokes of color. The stitches may be varied in size and in sequence, but the object of needlepoint remains the same — to cover all the canvas with wool stitches in such a fashion that you have a finished fabric of your own design, as tough as it is a proud possession.

Single or Double Canvas?

The scrim, or canvas, on which you work is generally made of cotton. There are two basic types of canvas, each of which comes in many sizes. Size here refers to the scale of the mesh. Larger mesh is covered with larger stitches, smaller mesh sizes with smaller stitches. The end use of a piece of needlepoint determines, in part, the choice of mesh size. But the opportunities for executing your own ideas and exploiting your skill are virtually unlimited as you find out how different types and sizes of canvas work.

If you go into a needlepoint shop to buy canvas — whether you intend to trace your own design on blank canvas or buy the design already painted on it — you will find a standard variety automatically offered to you. This is what is called mono canvas, or single-mesh canvas. It is usually white and just what the name implies: single strands of vertical threads interwoven with single strands of horizontal threads. Mono canvas is stiff and tends to be stubborn about relaxing as you work with it. But, being white, it accepts a painted design in color with such clarity, no wonder this is the choice of the needlepoint shops, whose purpose is to make the hobby of needlepoint as appealing as possible for the sake of the handsome sales it rings up.

To me, double canvas (Penelope is another name for it) is far preferable to single. Double canvas weaves "joined" pairs of vertical threads with double rows of horizontal threads. The vertical threads are not actually joined, but they are clearly visible as pairs, each two threads being close together and separated from

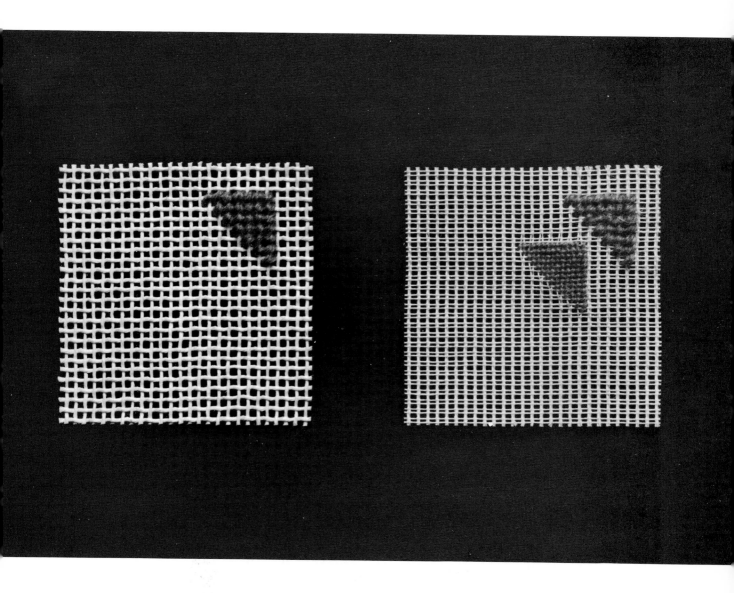

Mono or single canvas, and Penelope or double
canvas. Shown here in No. 10 mesh size (ten
stitches to the inch) and No. 10/20 (ten stitches
to the inch for gros point, twenty stitches when
split for petit point).

the next two by a slightly wider space. The horizontal threads are more equally spaced one from the next, but they, too, are paired in the weave. Double canvas is usually natural-color cotton rather than bleached white, though white Penelope has finally become available.

Double canvas offers you an option. You can cover crossed pairs of threads on the canvas; in other words, cover a joined pair of verticals and a pair of horizontals with each stitch, treating the pairs as if they were simply single strands of mono canvas. Or, you can pick out only one vertical thread and couple it with just one horizontal thread at the intersection. This smaller stitch, which is about one quarter the size of the larger, is known as petit point; the larger is called gros point. Doing petit point on double canvas is really to ignore the paired fashion in which the threads are woven and to stitch on the canvas as if it were a very fine mono canvas. (If you use mono canvas, the stitch qualifies as petit point when the mesh count is about sixteen to the inch or more, though there is no hard-and-fast rule about this.)

The many advantages of double canvas will be made clear later in this book. But to put it simply, double canvas enables you to work a very detailed subject in petit point and, rather than wasting time working acres of background in the same tiny stitch, to complete the background in the larger stitch. I find, also, that the stitches come out a little smoother when I use double canvas. Working double canvas in gros point, you are covering four threads with each stitch and the stitches are better padded than on mono canvas. On mono canvas, the yarn pulls tighter in each stitch because it is covering only two threads at a time and the stitches are not as plump and close together. To be sure, single mesh appears less complicated to work on. Keeping track of two crossed threads is easier at first sight than taking up the four threads of double canvas with each stitch. But once you get the feeling of double canvas, you forget all about this. You can only convince yourself by experience that double canvas gives the best results without any real extra trouble.

All those I have ever taught to do needlepoint have started on double canvas. When you start this way and later reach the stage of wanting to try your virtuosity at petit point, you are already accustomed to the double mesh you have to use. If you begin on single mesh, the chances are you will be intimidated by the double mesh and it will take time before you learn to put the needle in the right place.

Mesh Sizes of Canvas

When you buy canvas, you should know the numbering system for mesh sizes. Both mono and double canvas are numbered according to how many stitches you can be expected to work to the inch. For instance, No. 10 mono canvas has a mesh of ten threads to the inch, hence ten stitches to the inch. The corresponding double or Penelope canvas is numbered 10/20 because one inch can be covered in either ten gros-point stitches or twenty petit-point stitches.

Most of the canvases you would buy with the intention of making needlepoint pillows or upholstery are thirty-six inches wide. A rug is just a big piece of needle-point, and canvas for rugs is available up to forty inches wide. On rare occasions you will find rug canvas sixty inches wide, but few of us want to work on anything that big and bulky. The common forty-inch-wide rug canvas is No. 10, ten stitches to the inch.

The firm of Paternayan, which has a fascinating range of canvases imported from France, distributes canvas of ten, twelve, fourteen stitches to the inch, or even finer — as tiny as thirty-two stitches to the inch. The finer the canvas, the narrower it will be; No. 32 is only twenty-four inches wide. This firm has mono canvas in everything from ten to thirty-two stitches to the inch; in double canvas, Paternayan has every size from 10/20 to 16/32 in widths from eighteen inches to thirty-six inches. Good needlework-supply shops carry several of these canvases (see Shopping Information on page 183).

The finer the canvas you are willing to tackle, the more detail you can accomplish. It stands to reason that if you put twenty-four stitches to the inch instead of ten or twelve, you will be able to work in twice as much detail, or more. The decision depends on how much time and patience you are going to invest in the project. Larger mesh canvas covers twice as fast as the finer, but you will not be able to obtain subtle shading or great detail when you limit yourself to big stitches. However, you can do very effective big, bold designs on canvas as coarse as No. 10. The average beginner likes to be able to see that there is an end in sight when he starts a new project and it may be just as well not to try your patience too much at first.

Another factor in the choice of canvas is availability. No. 10 is the general, all-purpose, single-mesh canvas most people are familiar with. Most beginners start with it, though I personally feel that, if you are determined to start on single canvas, No. 12 gives more attractive results. No. 10/20 double-mesh canvas, the most common counterpart to No. 10 mono, is the one I recommend first for beginners. However, despite my personal preference, No. 10 and No. 12 single-mesh canvases are both all right for pillows, chair seats, piano-bench upholstery. Then, when you observe the good texture of the smaller stitch of No. 12, you will be tempted to improve on that, too, and to try No. 14 which I consider the best gauge of mono canvas. It is, however, somewhat harder to get than the others.

If you want more detail on a canvas of these mesh sizes, go to the equivalent in double mesh on which you can do some petit point. Unfortunately, gauges other than No. 10/20 are hard to find. I like to work twenty-four petit-point stitches to the inch on double canvas, but only a few places stock the appropriate No. 12/24 mesh size. There is a list of shops on page 183 where you can inquire. When I come across rare sizes of canvas, I buy five yards just to have it on hand. Some people like a No. 18 single-mesh canvas for terribly fancy work. This means eighteen stitches to the inch over the entire canvas, and that is a lot of stitching.

Still another type of canvas, known as Quick Point, is a coarse double-thread mesh meant for rugs. In my opinion, it is a waste of time to use this canvas because the stitch is so thick and coarse that the rug or whatever else you might make loses its identity as needlepoint. You would be better advised to use Quick Point canvas to hook a rug, for which it is excellent.

Most of the canvases we have described so far are thirty-six inches wide, cost up to eight dollars a yard, and are made of cotton or sometimes linen. There are also synthetic canvases. These are tough and springy and they stay that way. Working with them is like working with your hands full of razor blades. Most of the synthetic canvas you come across is in inexpensive kits assembled by manufacturers who think they have produced an easy way out of supplying the real thing. But anyone who appreciates handling the tools of needlepoint — the pliable canvas, the springy wool, the smoothly slipping needle — will be disenchanted with anything less than the best.

Needles

Needlepoint needles have long eyes and blunt points. The smallest (sizes 21, 22, 23 and 24) are petit-point needles. You would use one of these numbers to work on double canvases No. 10/20 through No. 16/32. The more stitches you plan to accomplish per inch, the finer needle you should choose. Gros-point needles are larger, and they are numbered 18, 19 and 20. A size 18 needle is the most common one to use for No. 10 to No. 14 canvas. It threads easily and is a good all-purpose needle. If you are making a needlepoint rug on No. 10 canvas, a size 15 needle is adequate. Size 13 needles are big, blunt instruments for working Quick Point rug canvas.

But in all the needlepoint I have done, I think I have used just three sizes of needle. The easiest way to choose a needle is to see how it threads. After you have chosen your canvas and wool, put the needle to the test. If you have trouble threading it (see page 37), it is too fine and you need a size lower in number. The finer the needle, the more pointed it will be, too. If you are working on a piece of petit point with too sharp a needle, you are very apt to prick your fingers. I prefer a short but blunt needle. There are commercial English needles on the market, called tapestry needles, which are blunt, but it makes more sense to purchase whatever needles the shop that is selling you the other materials has. In any case, if you buy the wrong size, needles cost only pennies.

Good needles are made of steel. In hot weather, and in moist hands, the steel needle will start to drag a bit as it is poked in and out of the canvas. You may not be aware of this at first; the work just gradually slows up. What has happened is that the surface of the needle has oxidized. If you have ever wondered about the little bags of sand attached to those tomato-shaped pin cushions that have been around forever (and are still available in the 5 & 10), this is where they come into their own. When the needle begins to drag, draw it back and forth through the little bag, and the oxidation is polished off.

You seldom buy needles by the package. A single needle will see you through any number of projects. In fact, the one I am currently using is on its fifteenth piece of petit point.

Needlepoint Wool

Needlepoint wool must be specially endowed to endure the tugging and pulling it is subjected to every time a stitch is made. The canvas is tough and abrasive to the wool, yet good needlepoint wool will, if anything, outlive the canvas. It is soft and pliable to work with. Handling it is a pleasure. So much more so than oil paint. You may feel at times that you would like to get into paint up to your elbows, but you cannot. You can literally get into wool up to your elbows.

One of the finest wools available in this country is Persian Rug Yarn. It is a product of Paternayan Brothers, and I generally refer to it as Paternayan wool or yarn. The most versatile of needlepoint yarns, it can be used as it comes, in strands of three threads loosely twisted together or "three-ply," for coarse stitching, or the strands can easily be pulled apart for one- or two-ply finer stitching. You simply lift one ply or thread away from the others. This yarn always works up evenly. Its slightly rough texture not only insures long wear but adds depth to the colors when the work is finished. The color range is adequate for all but the most minutely detailed project. There are three or four shades of each color.

A French yarn called Bon Pasteur, on the other hand, offers a seductive number of colors, as many as eighteen shades of red, for example, from pale pink to deep maroon (think of the apple you could paint in as many shades of oils). As you would expect, this yarn is important to anyone setting out to do very detailed modeling or shading. The basic colors are not as clear and usable as the three or four shades of each color of Paternayan yarn. Bon Pasteur is smoother than Paternayan. It is twisted in such a way that you have to develop a system for splitting it. The strand untwists and tends to snarl when you pull out one ply or thread, so that you have to keep retwisting and smoothing it out to split it again. This is not as easy as splitting Paternayan. I use Bon Pasteur yarn for shading in petit point when I want to make a figure or an object look sculptured. Not only the colors but the whole range of white to black comes in eighteen to twenty gradations. You can even make stone look like stone with it.

How much wool to buy is a question. It is all well and good to prepare a chart of how much wool may cover so much canvas. But I find people work so differently that one may use as much as a third more yarn on a given area than another because of working loosely. Others pull tightly and use far less yarn. My advice is to forget about trying to buy the exact amount of yarn you think you will need for a particular project. I believe in buying more than enough. Leftover wool from one project is inspiration for the next. Matching leftover colors, if you then need to reorder more, is no longer the problem it once was because most manufacturers have licked the differences in dye lots. But if you run short just a few strands before finishing a design, you may be hard put to find a shop that will sell you that little wool at a time.

Nor do you have to hesitate about storing needlepoint wool. Once upon a time, when it was excessively oily, you might as well have hung out a welcome sign to every moth in the neighborhood. Today, most wools are permanently moth-proofed. But, if you are undertaking large projects such as rugs, you may well prefer to buy wool in installments for other reasons. Wool for a 3′ x 5′ rug is a sizable investment, especially for the background color, which might sensibly be decided upon at a later date (see page 71).

Some people will be able to work on a canvas with the yarn three-ply just as it comes, others will peel off a thread and work with two-ply on the same mesh-size canvas. If you have trouble fitting one stitch in next to another, you are using a thicker strand of wool than the canvas can take. Or, if the canvas shows through the stitches, you may not be using enough threads in the strand. You must test the wool and canvas against your way of stitching to decide how many strands you should be using. When you work in the basketweave stitch, you will use about a third more wool than if you cover the canvas with the Continental stitch. (These stitches are described on page 33.)

Needlepoint wool is sold by weight. Though prices vary, 75¢ per ounce for Paternayan yarn is about what you can expect to pay. When you buy wool for a prepared canvas in a shop, you will see that the sales people quickly estimate by looking at the design roughly how much of each color you need. You will soon learn to do this yourself, for actually working needlepoint gives you a sense of how thick a hank of wool will cover how much canvas, and you learn to guess by eye that a hank of wool is about an ounce, or two ounces, or whatever. The whole process does remain guesswork, but most needlepointers are satisfied simply not to underestimate; leftover wool always finds a use eventually.

The important thing is to see all the colors, either by visiting needlepoint shops or sending to one of the sources on page 183 for a mailing of color samples. Through the mail you can expect two-inch samples of as many as 268 colors, which you can spread out in front of you and mix to your heart's content. You will probably get ideas just from looking at the colors. Or, if you have already decided on a design, you should see a good assortment of colors to find the best ones with which to work it out.

2 The Stitch

The basic stitch in needlepoint is one of the simplest in all needlework, and it never changes. Every stitch covers an intersection of one vertical thread and one horizontal thread of canvas, or an intersection of a pair of vertical threads and a pair of horizontal threads. Every stitch covers its intersection diagonally. The wool comes up from under the canvas through the hole at the lower left of the intersection; it crosses the intersection diagonally and upward, returning to the back of the canvas through the hole at the upper right of the intersection. No matter in what sequence you are placing stitches on the canvas, or how you may be skipping about to place your color where it belongs in the design, this diagonal direction of the stitch *never* changes from lower left to upper right over every intersection of threads on the canvas.

To get oriented once and for all on the direction of your stitch, the selvages of your canvas are always the up-and-down or vertical edges. On double canvas, the closely paired or "joined" threads always run up and down, too. With the vertical direction of your canvas thus clearly established, the lower left-hand corner and the upper right-hand corner of the canvas become the points that indicate the diagonal direction of all the stitches for the whole canvas.

Note, however, that you can turn your canvas around and still have the stitches going in the right direction. What you do is turn the canvas *completely* around, so that the edge that was at the bottom is at the top. The left-to-right stitches will all remain in the same diagonal direction. What you must *not* do is turn the canvas half way around, so that what were the vertical sides of the canvas are at the top and bottom. If you do this, different areas of work will eventually join up in a herringbone of opposing diagonals. This is against the law. Take it all out. There will be reasons, explained later, for turning the canvas around, so remember when

you do this that you must turn it all the way, upside-down, so that what was the upper-right corner becomes the lower-left corner, and vice versa, and you will have no trouble.

The sequence in which you put the stitches on canvas makes the difference between what are known as the Continental stitch and the basketweave stitch. Both stitches look the same when the needlepoint is finished, the individual stitches all coming out in the same diagonal direction. It is the direction of the *rows* along which the stitches are taken that is different.

The Continental stitch is a horizontal or vertical (or sometimes "back-stitched" diagonal) sequence of stitches in a single line, broken or unbroken. The stitches are placed in rows corresponding to the horizontal or vertical threads of the canvas. This is the equivalent in needlepoint of rows of knitting.

The basketweave stitch derives its name from the pattern the stitches make on the back of the canvas. They look no different on the front, or face, of the canvas. The stitches are placed along diagonal rows of intersections of canvas threads. The rows of intersections are straight, but at a 45-degree angle to the vertical and horizontal threads of the canvas.

If you are a beginner, do not try to follow the directions in this chapter in your mind's eye. Get out a piece of canvas, needle, and wool, and practice in a far corner of the canvas. With the real thing in front of you, you can then see plainly how simply these needlepoint stitches work.

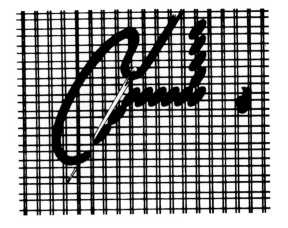

Continental stitch

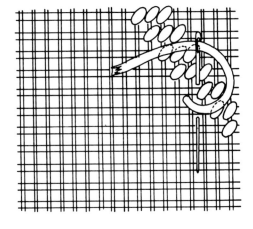

Basketweave stitch

The Continental Stitch

On a corner of canvas, block off a square one inch by one inch. For the Continental stitch, you will first work a row from right to left along the top of the square. Pull needle and thread up through the next-to-last hole in the top right-hand corner of the square. Then insert the needle in the hole above and to the right (in other words, you are crossing an intersection diagonally, as explained before). Pull the stitch flat, and bring the needle up again through the hole immediately to the left of the hole you began with. Believe it or not, the wool will now be in position for this sequence of steps to be repeated. Continue to the end of the top of the one-inch square. Now turn the canvas completely around, so the stitched row at the top of the square is at the bottom. Work another row of stitches from right to left in exactly the same way, parallel to and just next to the first row of stitches. When you get back to the end of the inch, turn the canvas all the way round again, and keep stitching and turning until you have filled in the one-inch square.

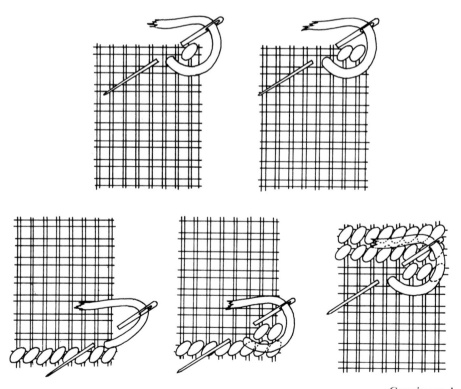

Continental stitch

The Basketweave Stitch

In another one-inch square of the canvas, experiment with the basketweave stitch. Begin the same way, at the top right-hand corner, and make the first two stitches from right to left, exactly the same as for beginning the Continental stitch. But, instead of continuing to the left horizontally, for the third stitch pull the needle up through the hole directly *under* the hole you began with. The wool will now be in position to complete this third stitch over the intersection directly under the first stitch. Now, under the third stitch is another intersection; over this you make the fourth stitch. Then bring your needle up in the hole that will allow you to make stitch number five over the intersection just to the left of the third stitch. Yes, you are climbing upward. The next stitch is number six, to be taken to the left of number two. You have arrived back at the top edge of the one-inch square. Take yet another stitch to the left along the top edge. Then work your way back down, "southeast" so to speak, all the way down the diagonal that is now clearly emerging. You then come back up the diagonal again, which you can think of, if it helps, as working "northwest."

You are building a pyramid in which the stitches of one row dovetail neatly between the stitches of the previous row. The pyramid gradually increases until you have reached the full diagonal dimension of the one-inch square, at which point the lengths of the rows will be decreased, instead of increased, in order to fill in the second triangle-shaped half of the square. Note that you have not once had to turn the canvas around. This is one of the several advantages of the basketweave stitch. When you flip over the sample bit of canvas, you will see on the back the amazing pattern of basketweave. It looks like old-fashioned monk's cloth.

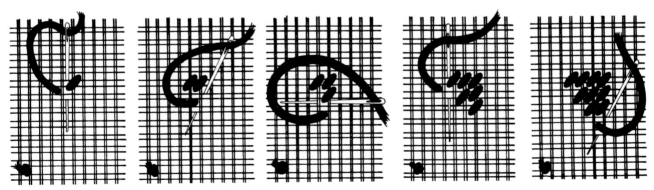

Basketweave stitch

Which Stitch to Use

The Continental and basketweave stitches each have their uses. The stitches are, in method, very distinct from each other if you are covering an area of any size. But you may find when you are working small irregular areas, for shading or for a small pattern in your design, that you lose track of just which one you *are* using. This does not really matter, providing every stitch is put in on its proper lower-left to upper-right diagonal and providing you are not using too much of the Continental stitch, as is explained below.

What is the advantage of puzzling out the basketweave? For one thing, it becomes more interesting to do than the Continental stitch once you have mastered it. For another, the more basketweave on your canvas, the less the canvas will be pulled out of shape. In fact, a piece of needlepoint done entirely in the Continental stitch will almost certainly become badly distorted. It is many times harder to block to bring it back to the original intended shape, and it may have to be blocked four or five times. There is a diagonal pull so strong on the canvas that, however beautifully blocked, it may still "walk" back out of shape eventually. Only when you have had a carefully measured piece of canvas mounted, and then seen it suddenly revert to the crooked thing it was before you blocked it, do you realize it would have been worth the effort to learn the basketweave stitch in the first place.

But both styles of stitching are useful, each in its own way. The only time you should use the Continental stitch is for putting in a single row of stitches, in any given direction. Single rows of stitches outlining areas of different colors are very useful in plotting both flat designs and gradations of shading. The areas should then be filled in with basketweave. When you reach the chapter on repeat patterns, you will see specific uses for the Continental stitch — in plotting the verticals and horizontals of a caning motif, for example. But notice that the small spaces of color that give depth and reality to that motif, and stability to the finished fabric, are filled in with basketweave. As you become proficient in needlepoint, it is desirable to fashion as much basketweave per block of design as possible, even for something "realistic" and complicated such as a frond of a plant. An almost freehand use of basketweave is the test of a topnotch needlepointer.

(You may hear elsewhere of another needlepoint stitch, the half-cross stitch, which also looks like the Continental and basketweave stitches on the face of the canvas. I do not recommend it for two reasons. It gives inadequate wool padding on the back of the canvas, and it cannot be made to work well on mono canvas or for petit point.)

The Continental and basketweave stitches are made exactly the same way for petit point as for gros point. An embroidery hoop may be helpful for intricate work in petit point. There are elaborate frames made for embroidery to keep the twill taut so that stitches stay aligned, but I prefer an ordinary embroidery hoop. It keeps the necessary area of canvas flat, so that you do not have to strain to hold it taut while you work, ending up with cramped fingers. Some people work all their needlepoint on big wooden frames, but the trouble with a frame is that you have to lean it up against something, and then you have to turn the whole thing over every time you end one piece of wool and start another on the back of the canvas.

How to Begin — the Work Plan

Let us suppose you have prepared your canvas as directed on page 64. Now, to thread the needle, fold a strand of yarn over the sharp edge of the head of the needle, and pull it down tight over the needle. Pinch the yarn between thumb and forefinger as you withdraw the needle. Still pinching the strand of wool in one hand, feed the doubled yarn into the long eye of the needle. Pull the doubled strand through the eye, and then release one end of the strand so that you have a short doubled strand near the head. Make a knot at the long end.

Insert needle and yarn from the *front* of the canvas through a hole about an inch and a half away from where you plan to make your first stitch. The knot will hold it in place. As you stitch, you will work over, or cover up, the inch and a half of tail in back to the knot, at which point you lop off the knot with scissors. No knots are ever allowed to remain in finished needlepoint!

To finish off the strand of yarn, on the back of the canvas weave a short length of it through the backs of about ten or fifteen stitches, away from the last stitch you have made; then weave it back again toward the same stitch, and clip it off. The wool will be locked in and can never pull out. Now that you have an area of stitches started, instead of starting a new strand of wool with a knotted tail as you did before, weave the new wool on the back a little distance *away* from that same last stitch and then back to it again, locking the strand just as you did the one you just finished off. Now come up through the canvas to the front, through the hole where you will make your next stitch.

When you are starting out on your first piece of needlepoint, I would advise a few practice rows of background to develop confidence before plunging into the central design motif. (Repeat patterns in the background are something else again, and these are dealt with in another chapter.) Do only a sample area, however. A long time ago I read that it is always wiser to work from the center motif outward in all directions. I didn't quite understand why. Then I worked a whole background area around a center motif, I don't remember what it was, which I left until last. This was to be done in petit point. What happened was, all the sides filled in with wool pushed toward the middle, leaving a blob of canvas in the center that was like a mass of spaghetti to work with; I had a great deal of trouble organizing stitches. Working in the reverse way, center motif first, the center holds firm, and when you work the background the edges of the canvas pull back flat. Another reason to wait before beginning the background is that you may not want to decide on the color for it right away.

If canvas shows through any finished areas as you work, chances are you are not using heavy enough yarn to cover it, or you are pulling too tight. Now, while you are practicing on the background, is the time to correct whatever is wrong. However, if, after you finish a piece, you see some thin spots in the stitching, you can work back over them with a single or double ply of wool (more about repairs on page 43). Try to develop your own rhythm, remembering that you are "laying on" the wool to cover the surface of the canvas in as even and flat a way as possible. You will discover the method most comfortable for you. Do not, in any case, be discouraged by an uneven surface of stitches. Blocking and steaming later on will fuzz up the yarn to a degree and help smooth the surface by evening up the stitches.

Your work plan now begins with the central motif, and it is a good idea to start in the middle of it. However, when the motif covers most of the total space of the canvas, you do not have to start in the absolute center. If, for example, you are doing one of the sun faces on page 156 or 159, you might begin with the rays at the right of the canvas and then gradually work into the expression lines of the face.

In working the design, the best procedure is to outline each of the areas of color with the Continental stitch, filling them in as you go with the basketweave stitch. In outlining the areas, you will soon notice that the stitches are easy to place when the direction of the outline is vertically downward, or horizontally from right to left, or diagonally either to the right or to the left. But when you need to go up vertically or from left to right horizontally to follow the outline, you suddenly feel stranded, somehow you aren't clear on how to take the next stitch. This is because the Continental stitch just won't go upward or to the right; what you must do is turn the canvas upside down (as you did at the end of a row in practicing a solid area of the Continental stitch; page 34). Now you can continue around your outline upside down, and the stitches can accumulate downward or across to the left again without trouble.

There are certain things you should watch out for from the beginning. It is always a good idea to try to work each strand of yarn to the end rather than wind up with leftover bits of wool six or eight inches long. Short strands like this may be perfectly good to use for a half dozen stitches, but they are so short you will probably throw them away instead. I work a strand of yarn as far as I can, even if I have to skip to another space to continue the color. If the area in between is empty and not very large, you can simply skip, across the back of the canvas, to the point where you want to start the color again. (Later, the filling in of the empty area will cover the short strand of loose wool on the back.) If the area in between is filled in, always weave your color under the backs of the stitches to your new starting point, so that no loose strands will remain on the back of the finished needlepoint. Of course, if the jump is a long one, it is best to lock the strand, cut it off, and use the remainder elsewhere if you can. Among needle-pointers, any flagrant waste of yarn is considered unprofessional.

You may find, in trying to skip the shortest possible distances between small neighboring areas of the same color of basketweave, that the areas tend to get filled up from right to left and downward, leaving spaces to be filled toward the upper left or right that seem rather a long leap away. You can do here with the basketweave just what you do in outlining with the Continental stitch; turn the canvas upside down and the areas, wrong side up, will be much easier to get at.

When you are ready to fill in the background (and every time I say fill in, I mean with basketweave), start at the upper right-hand corner of your canvas and work toward the center. When you meet the center motif, you will have to split your background work areas in order not to skip back and forth over the back of the finished design. Work down the right side to the lower right-hand corner, then leftward from there as far as background stitching and center design continue to meet. When the background is ready to shoot past the design at the far left, stop.

Now go back to the top and pick up the background where you left off, starting the first new row of the background color next to the center motif, or at the point where you took the last background stitch. Work the basketweave to the far left-hand corner and then down the left-hand side, until you reach the point where the background on this side meets the unfinished background at the bottom. Then all you have left to fill in is the far left-hand corner.

The diagram below shows how you progress from one area to the next on the background, going from area 1 through 4. You could make one change in this sequence, doing area 3 across the top before doing area 2 across the bottom. There are two reasons why you should follow this plan in working backgrounds. First, when a row of background stitches hits the central design, you do not want

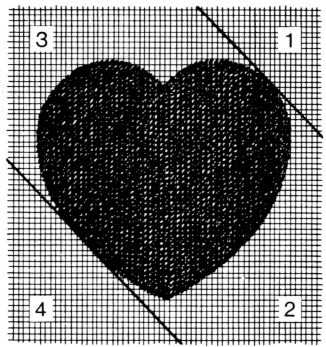

Sequence for working backgrounds

to skip across the back of the design to get to the other side of it, as this would leave loose loops of wool on the back of the canvas. The other reason is a little more complicated: by following this work plan, you are assured of keeping the smooth texture of the basketweave at the points where you stop and start the background areas. It could be a temptation, for instance, to turn the canvas upside-down to start corner 4 of the background. Don't do it, for the chances are the basketweave will not mesh properly on the back when the areas of background meet, so that, even though the diagonal of the stitches on the front will be correct, there will nevertheless be a diagonal ridge in the texture of the needlepoint that will always show. So, though I have said you can turn the canvas around for convenience in most circumstances, for backgrounds of any considerable area this is a bad idea. If your piece of needlepoint is designed to be almost all motif and practically no background, then you can turn the canvas if you want; the irregular ridge will barely show, if at all.

If your central motif is done in petit point, there is one more thing you need to know about working the background. Your petit-point stitches, in theory, take up in blocks of four stitches the spaces that would otherwise be taken up by gros-point stitches made over the double mesh. But, in practice, the delicate outline of the petit-point motif will not have covered every one of the paired threads of the split mesh. Therefore, when the gros-point background abuts with the petit-point motif, there will be tiny petit-point spaces left over in spots around the edge of the motif. Go back after you have filled in as much gros-point background as the double mesh will take, and fill in the empty petit-point spaces with petit-point stitches done in the background color, splitting the yarn as you did for the motif.

Mistakes and Repairs

After you have completed a couple of pieces of needlepoint, you will have developed a kind of stitch rhythm. The stitches get to be very neat. But if in the beginning you are a little tense, some stitches may be too tight, or maybe you are a little tight and the stitches are a bit too loose. The difference in the tension of the stitches makes for an uneven surface though this may not be as bad as you think at first.

It is somewhat difficult to tighten up loose stitches if you have many of them. Unless you can catch yourself in time and pull the yarn back stitch by stitch, you may have to take your chances on leaving the loose stitches as they are. They are not as common as tight stitches. When stitches are tight, the canvas shows through. But you can work back over them and, if you do it carefully, you will never see there are two layers of stitches. Use a single- or double-ply strand (a strand thinner than what you used originally may be best) and pull a little tighter than you do with an ordinary stitch. Wool is flexible.

If you have put in a few stitches you do not want, do not try to insert the needle back into the spaces through which you pulled it up, because you may get entangled with wool from other stitches. It is much easier to unthread the needle, turn the canvas over, and pull the last stitch out from the back; then turn the canvas back again, and pull the yarn through to the front. Keep pulling stitches and flipping your canvas, using the head of the needle as a tool to loosen the stitches.

In the event you discover quite an area that you do not want (maybe you have done a section of stitches in the wrong direction), you will have no choice but to cut it out with scissors. This is tricky. When you put a pair of sharp little scissors in there and start to cut, be careful. If you meet with the least resistance, it probably means you are cutting canvas. This can happen. If you should cut a strand of canvas, you can lay in a new strand. Just peel off a thread from the edge of the canvas and lay it over the strand you cut. Then rework needlepoint over it.

When you clip out an area of stitches, you must, for every color involved, stop a number of stitches short of the area you want to get rid of. Now, instead of cutting, pull out the remainder of the offending stitches with the head of your needle until you have a tail of yarn long enough to thread and weave into stitches on the back of the canvas. All the cut colors must be locked in in this way, or stitches will pull out later and cut ends of yarn will stick right out of the canvas. Then retrace your steps carefully over the canvas, correcting whatever it was you did wrong.

If you do serious damage to the canvas, if a dog chews on your needlepoint, or whatever, don't worry, you can patch. It is not too hard to put a piece of canvas over the torn place and to stitch over the two layers. First clear away stitches around the torn place so that you have a rim of undamaged canvas; cut the stitches out and lock in all the tails of yarn. Then just be sure to keep the mesh of the two layers of canvas lined up with each other. The replacement stitches will look exactly the same size from the top, or face, as they do on a single layer of canvas.

Once I realize I have made a mistake, I would often rather try to make it part of the design than change it. Maybe the owl's eyes are a little bulgier than I thought they were going to be, or maybe the beak is a little too long. It seems safer to make the owl's now rather odd expression part of the design than to take the chance of wrecking it. If a starfish turns out to have six arms, why not? Let it. Nobody ever sees your mistakes. Anybody who does needlepoint is just happy to see someone else doing it too. Those that don't do it are so impressed with all those stitches that they never pick a thing apart.

These few pages of instructions are even more than you need to know to begin your first piece of needlepoint. As you become more proficient, the descriptions of how various designs in this book were worked will give you ideas for how to move about your canvases to execute more and more complicated designs. But there are few hard-and-fast rules — really only the hints and warnings given here. Half the fun is discovering your own way of doing things neatly and efficiently — and with more and more basketweave!

3 Designing Your Own

Until about fifteen years ago, people who did needlepoint in this country usually bought it with the center design already worked, and it was usually a bouquet with a few petit-point stitches added gratuitously to the centers of flowers and the veins of leaves to make the canvas look like a lot more for the money. Filling in the background was considered doing needlepoint. (It was different in Europe where people have always wanted to work their own designs.) Needlepoint was almost entirely a flower medium then. The familiar matching sets of dining-chair seats, which you can still buy today, were fair game for needlepointers, and everyone did them with black or at least dark backgrounds. I think one of the reasons for these somber colors was that women worked on those sets for years; black was probably safest because colors changed character by the time all the needlepoint was finished.

But now there has been a complete shift of interest. Just about everyone wants to do more than fill in backgrounds, and all of a sudden designs for needlepoint are being conjured up from all over the place — from grocery shelves ("pop" Campbell's soup cans), museums of natural history (animal pelts, autumn leaves), and all manner of printed material, including postcards from abroad and record albums from home. Our attitude toward what is a proper subject for needlepoint is far less reverent than it was, and there is no doubt this tempts many more people into doing needlepoint. The fact that we can now buy a variety of glorious wool colors has a lot to do with the current enthusiasm too.

The needlepoint we are doing today is as different from the filled-in flower motifs of the past as day is from night. Sets of chair seats are certainly still fair game, but not repeating the identical motif over and over — not if you are going to have to live through copying it again and again yourself! I do not think I could do two, let alone six or eight, chair seats exactly the same. But a series of variations on one theme can be very diverting, such as — not to be too wildly offbeat — a collection of fruits for dining-room chairs. Why not pomegranates for one, great big tangerines for another, and so on and on? Even if you must choose roses, there is no reason why you cannot vary them, from big floppy cabbage roses to tight little tea roses. At least each one will be a different project in its own right.

And so, with so much freedom to choose, how are you going to make up your mind what to do? Consider first what subject matter appeals to you, what you want to make, how much detail you are up to, and whether designing your own isn't more likely to produce exactly what *you* want.

Some people enjoy doing needlepoint mechanically, stitching away without thinking too much about what they are doing. They are happy with a design made of big broad areas of color because it does not require a great deal of concentration nor even too frequent changes of wool colors. A large background area doesn't bother them at all.

I know one person who has very particular requirements for the ideal needlepoint design. It must have a portion of complicated detail for hard thinking; another portion of pattern that is interesting but easier to do; and then plain areas for mindless relaxation — something for every mood all on the same piece.

But the people who fascinate me are the ones who get so hooked on what can be done with needlepoint that their designs fill more and more space and the plain areas shrink to almost nothing. To them, the mechanical way of stitching, just because it is so simple, is terribly boring. I know any number of people who have exploded their central motif to such a point that there is practically no background left, and yet they still ask me if I know anyone they "can hire to fill in the background cheap."

What to Make First

I suggest a pillow as your first project for many reasons. You can keep it if it turns out beautifully, but there is no problem about giving it away if you aren't too happy with it. If you go to the trouble, for instance, of shaping a piece of needlepoint to upholster a chair, then you are going into something special that will only fit your own chair. When you get into something as involved as a rug, you are talking money. Either upholstery or a rug is intimidating because you desperately want it to be right for that particular chair or that particular space. But a simple square or circle of a pillow is not intimidating. You are not even working on anything of a particular size, as you can make it bigger as you go along, or change the shape, or make it smaller if you decide you don't like the background color. A pillow is completely flexible. Most important, I think, you become more deeply involved in the design itself than in what it will be used for. Even small projects such as handbags and eyeglasses cases, for which the shape is as important as the design, create limitations you don't have with a pillow. When you get to be an expert and experiment with really difficult designs, you may end up doing nothing *but* pillows.

Your Own Theme for Subject Matter

Just in case you should get hooked on needlepoint, why not start with a theme that can be kept going as long as you want? A sound idea for this could be just things not necessarily related in any way except that you happen to like them. I have one seat cushion in my apartment that could well have been a set of a dozen different pillows. The subjects represented on it (color picture 10) all are simply favorite things of mine — chipmunks, shells, mushrooms, frogs, holly — done together instead of separately. If you are doing needlepoint for your own home, a collection of your favorite things will be subjects you will want to live with for a while. Or choose subjects that appeal especially to someone you may want to give your needlepoint to. Giving needlepoint away is one of the chief reasons for doing needlepoint at all.

In the beginning you will do fairly simple renderings of whatever most intrigues you. The important thing is that the inspiration for your first and future needlepoint projects be things you do care about, because your enthusiasm for working on something that matters to you in some special way will come through in the finished product. And find the right source material from which to design the needlepoint, too. If you want to paint a flower in needlepoint, please find a picture of a flower you really like, not just any flower. If you like anemones, don't settle for daisies. If you like butterflies, find a good butterfly print to adapt to needlepoint. Do not take just any butterfly design that comes along.

Another word of advice on the choice of a motif. Be sure at first that what you pick is comparatively simple in coloring. I am not suggesting that you limit yourself to any specific number of colors. If you have the nerve and perseverance, you can be as adventurous as you like with color. But in the beginning it is best to be reasonable. I would not want anyone to trace off a design, transfer it to canvas, and have it turn out a big pot of bouillabaisse with some 100 colors to place. You might say: "Where do I start? Which are the colors I picked out two weeks ago that I thought were going to do that? Is it this red or is it that red, or maybe I meant orange?" You may scare yourself. It is a lot wiser to pick something that does not involve too many colors. But, just as you pick a favorite subject, pick favorite colors to start you off on a first project.

Why Design Your Own?

When I propose that you design your own needlepoint, I do not for a moment mean to discount the fact that today you can get excellent designs at needlepoint shops. They are getting better and better. But what most people do not realize is that they can do perfectly good designs themselves by borrowing the elements they want from here and there — which is just what most of the shops do. You pay a fancy price for designs painted on canvas in needlepoint shops. You are not paying this for the canvas and wool, which are relatively inexpensive, but for the designs. There is absolutely no comparison in price when you design your own. And then it is yours, nobody else has it, it is completely personal. When you are all through, there is so much more satisfaction in having started out from scratch with an idea of your own than there is working over somebody else's design. But don't take it from me. Try it yourself.

Subjects and Sources, and How to Use This Book

Since the first step in designing your own needlepoint is selecting the motif, you need to find sources. There are some very good familiar sources, some uncommon sources, and some *non*-sources. Before I go on to describe the possibilities, let me point out the obvious, that this book is itself intended to serve as a source of designs. As I explain further on, photostating is the principal method of picking up designs from books or other printed sources. There is every reason to do the same with any photograph in this book, whether color or black-and-white, if you see something you want to copy or adapt. You will simply be using needlepoint as a source for needlepoint, and it will work extremely well, especially when you also have the original color picture to refer to as you stitch. The processes of tracing and transferring to canvas will be exactly the same as for using any other source. My only word of warning about this is that you must not burden yourself with the idea that a needlepoint source can, or should, be copied stitch for stitch (unless it is a special design such as the repeat patterns in Chapter 6). I will say over and over that no design can nor should be copied exactly, and that goes for needlepoint designs too.

  As is evident from their captions, the line drawings in this book are drawn to be photostated up to workable sizes. They are intended to provide a capsule source book that will give you ideas about various types of designs and projects for which you decide on your own color schemes. Chapter 12, "Coloring Your Own," has drawings and advice to help beginners in particular get started on designing their own.

Among the standard good sources for needlepoint designs are wallpapers, slip-cover, upholstery and drapery fabrics, and dress materials, all of which can inspire needlepoint. They are good because the commercial designer has had to simplify the motif for practical reasons before it is printed. Wallpaper showrooms are great stockpiles of designs. Your own home might well turn up a motif you want to adapt from curtains or slipcovers, from a patterned tablecloth or an area rug.

There is, however, no good reason to duplicate any motif exactly as it appears in the fabric or wallpaper or rug. You might as well cover the pillow in the same material. Instead, take a few pears from a paisley print, for example, and arrange them in a circle or a square, or plant one big one in the center of the pillow with a few little ones around it. Take one or two poppies from a curtain of wall-to-wall poppies and do them, oversize, on the pillow. The fabric or wallpaper or rug is your crib sheet. The idea is to crib some of the shapes and rearrange them as you like on the canvas. As long as you repeat the basic shape that is in the original, the relationship will be there when you put the pillow in the room with the poppy curtains. The design will not look so "happy-hands-at-home" if you relax and repeat only the basic shape rather than try to duplicate the exact overall design. That is the point of this chapter and, for that matter, of this book. Your needle-point design should be your re-interpretation of something as you want to use it. There is no satisfaction in doing dead ringers.

Design talent is not a prerequisite. You can crib all you want. Just make up your mind not to be too literal about it (which is difficult anyway), and your adaptation is bound to have its own originality. You can trace a motif right off a fabric and take the colors from it too. As a matter of fact, the tracing paper itself helps you to edit the design. When you place the tracing paper over the fabric, you will be able to see only the most distinct lines, so you cannot help adapting the motif as you trace it. You can also trace a flower from one fabric, leaves from another, and put the two tracings together. It is amazing to see what happens when you play around with various fragments of designs. You could even just take circular paper cutouts of different sizes and colors. Draw an outline of your pillow on tracing paper, drop the circles on it, and then move them around within the outline. I defy you not to hit a point where you will think it looks kind of pretty. Stop right there, and trace the whole thing off. Similarly, you could trace paisley pears from one fabric and flowers from another, lay one tracing over another and move them around until you like the composition, then make a final single tracing overall.

Another possibility is completely to change the scale of a design. The butterflies in the pillow tracing on page 53 were reduced to barely half the size of those in the original rug design on page 165. Or, they could be tiny, done in petit point the size you see them on the page, and rearranged in a different pattern as well.

Among *non*-sources for needlepoint design are photographs of rooms in perspective or rugs in perspective or, for that matter, butterflies on the wing in perspective. These are not good sources to crib from. Why? Because you want to paint the design head on, so you can see the object as it is, not distorted by perspective. Close-up documentary pictures don't distort and are by far the best, whether the subject is flora or fauna or floor tile. Most china patterns leave me cold, either on or off the china, but some classic porcelain motifs make very good needlepoint designs. Modern rug designs may seem like a good source, but I consider them non-sources because you can do much better in books than in most rug showrooms. Gift-wrap papers and most greetings cards, with some exceptions, are pretty poor designs in themselves, let alone for the labor of needlepoint.

As for paintings, do not attempt to reproduce in needlepoint what an accomplished artist has created in oils. Find inspiration in the shapes and colors of a Braque or a Matisse, but do not try to make like Matisse in needlepoint. I am sure most artists would set fire to themselves if they ever saw how people have interpreted their paintings in needlepoint. I have seen adaptations of Van Gogh that would stand your hair on end. If you could match every brush mark stitch by stitch, it might come off and it might be great. But when you trace and then when you start to stitch, you start changing, eliminating details. You almost *have* to go wrong. It is far better to take pointers from paintings about composition, to take elements you like and adapt them in your own way. There is no sense to an inaccurate (or even accurate) facsimile of art. The idea is to make a lovely thing of your own that is pretty to look at in its own right.

52   *Paisley pillow. The various pieces of this design*
      were traced from the paisley rug design in color
      picture 39 and rearranged in a new composition
      to make a fifteen-inch-square pillow. From the
      tracing of the rug on page 163 you could
      assemble still other fragments for pillow-size
      paisley designs. Paisley patterns are ideal for
      making up your own color schemes.

Butterfly pillow. The original design for this, taken from the same fabric as the rug in color picture 40, had enormous butterflies which reduced well for this fourteen-inch pillow.

What I have used as much as anything else for souce material is European post-cards. If you travel, you can hardly buy better, more inexpensive photographs. If the photograph depicts a section of pavement or a piece of statuary or an animal quite close up, the "editing" has already been done for you. You have the picture blown up by photostat, then trace the parts you want and outline them on canvas. When you are ready to start to work, you have this marvelous little original, the postcard, to carry with you as reference. It becomes your color card.

Catalogues and announcements from art galleries are often good uncommon sources. So are travel circulars. Photographs you take yourself can be equally inspiring. I always have a Minox camera with me in Europe. I did one pillow of a wonderful little fountain in the Piazza Colonna in Rome (two dolphins and a great shell, page 136) from one of my Minox shots. I have never seen another photograph of it. One of the beauties of taking your own photographs is that you can have enlargements made from the negatives instead of having photostats made for tracing. The original snapshot, like the postcard, then becomes your portable guide.

Nowadays, record-album covers can be unexpected sources for needlepoint designs. The tiger pillow I worked in petit point (color picture 28) was lifted right from the jacket of a record album. Illustrated children's books are great too.

For realistic interpretations of growing things, seed catalogues turn up faithful illustrations for you to copy or blow up and trace in a composition. Of the custom designs I have drawn lately, eighty per cent of the requests have been for flowers. I hate needlepoint flowers, I suppose because they have been done so much. I never made a record of the first flower pillow I designed at the request of a friend in Florida, and to this day I would deny designing it if anybody asked me. But I have had to make a compromise with my own feelings, and anyway, even flowers need not be used in listless compositions. One design I liked doing was the crossed ram's horns (color picture 4) stuffed with an odd assortment of flowers, wheat, and miscellaneous plant materials.

I have found that three or four books are all you need for as much horticultural material as you could ever possibly use. The *National Geographic* has published a wonderful book on garden fruits and flowers. Recently, an English concern exported a book illustrating every possible species of rose. It is a treasure trove for needlepointers who like roses.

Some sources of design motifs are timeless. Meyer's book on classical design, one of the best, is in paperback, and it is the all-time classic. These and other books crammed with basic source material are listed on page 187. The pictures are often small, but the wealth of detail will all become useable once you have your chosen motif blown up by photostat. In four or five of these books there would be enough needlepoint motifs to keep you busy the rest of your life.

If you are looking for good geometric border motifs, I would not recommend books on interior decoration or architecture because, like magazine ads, you get pictures of whole rooms in perspective. One of the best sources is catalogues from tile companies. I have an excellent one of Portuguese tiles that I use frequently. If you are interested in geometric patterns, you can make up your own from any number of sources. There are wonderful children's games that involve parts you can manipulate to make geometric designs. If more conventional herringbone, checked, plaid, hound's-tooth designs appeal to you, dress fabrics and, sometimes, in bolder versions, slipcover and upholstery fabrics are worth investigating. I have designed some simple repeat patterns which you will find in Chapter 6.

Fool-the-eye designs are fun to work out in needlepoint — marble patterns, wood grains, animal skins, tortoise shell, and so forth. See Chapters 7 and 8 for line drawings of such patterns that have been included in this book. You can have them photostated to the size you want directly from the printed page and for several of them there are color pictures in the book to use for color guides. But there are many more patterns that you could try. For marbles, look in the 5 & 10 or a paint-supply store where peel-and-stick papers are sold by the yard. More can be found in catalogues from any marble supplier. Wood grains of all sorts are available in wallpapers, and since these have already been exaggerated for effect, you can copy them more easily than the grain of wood in a piece of furniture (or see color picture 23). For fur skins, good pictures may be found in books on animals, many foreign magazines, and, as I mentioned before, occasionally on record jackets, postcards, and travel posters.

There is almost no subject you cannot find by looking in books. They are your best source for uncommon material to trace. Some books may be fairly special and lurking on the shelves of the public library. Most libraries will permit you to make a tracing if you place a sheet of ciear stiff plastic (available in art-supply stores) over the page you are tracing. Do not be shy about asking permission.

Symbolic motifs that may have special meaning to you may be found in some of the books listed on page 187. For instance, you will find coats of arms, flags of all nations, versions of the American eagle, the British lion, the French fleur-de-lys, the Aztec sun. Blazoning arms and ensigns of heraldry are also in print for you to crib from freely for needlepoint for posterity.

Numerals and letters of the alphabet are musts for the library of the needle-pointer. From a book of lettering you can design special petit-point monograms for friends and family, but perhaps even more important is the signing of your own work. Everybody owes it to himself to sign his needlepoint. Not only is so much time and effort worthy of your signature, it is a good check on which piece you completed before another piece. You should exercise judgment in signing. I generally work my initials and the date in a corner of the background, just a shade different from the background color and usually in petit point. If friends pick up the pillow and think they see a mistake, I simply tell them to hold it in a good light and they will see it is the initials and a date. Often I work the initials of the person to whom I am giving the needlepoint just above my own. The two sets of initials and the date form a neat block in a corner of the canvas. As a starter, you can pick up initials from the alphabets on pages 57 and 58.

But I also advise against signing a piece of needlepoint prematurely! A friend of mine set out to do an enormous project, a 10′ x 12′ rug in three or four sections. The design was barely started when I found her signing one piece with *fecit*, Latin for "made by" or "by the hand of", with her initials and the current date. I suggested she postdate this thing by about ten years. She got mad, but she took it all out and ended up signing the rug seven years later in a rather conservative way in the corner.

Photostating

You can change the size of any design or motif by taking it to a shop that does photostatic enlargements. You may want to blow up a picture or a section of a picture in order then to trace the larger version. Or you may already have made a tracing, from a book or section of wallpaper or fabric, which you want enlarged. (Make the tracing in ink with a fine-line marker.) For that matter, you can have things reduced in size, too, if you want. In any case, the change in size has to be

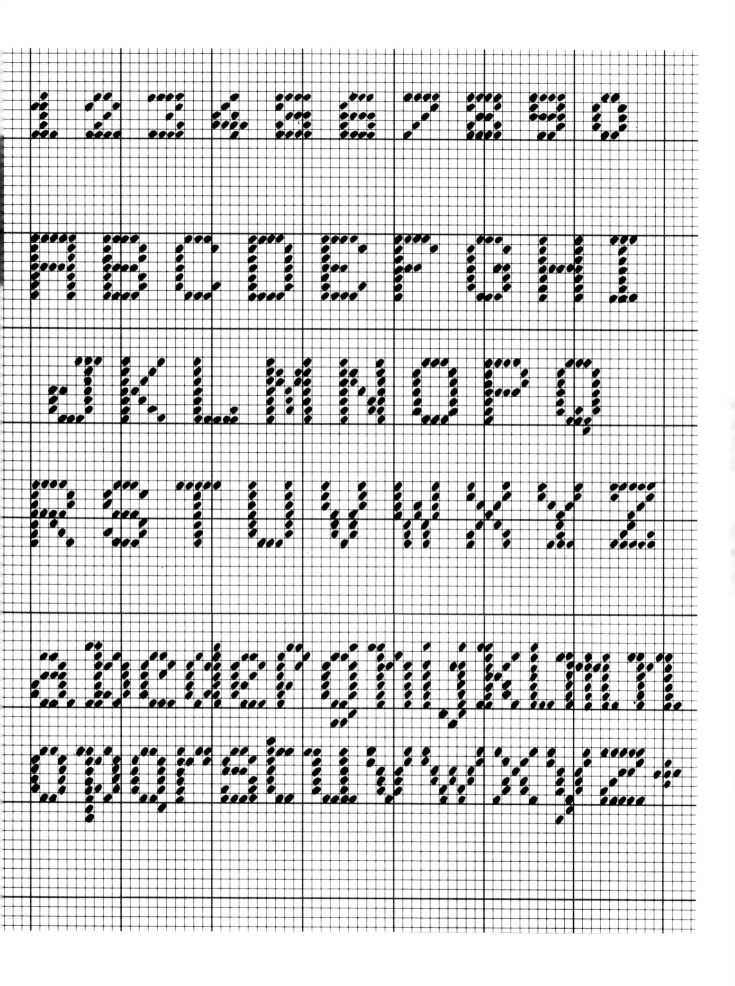

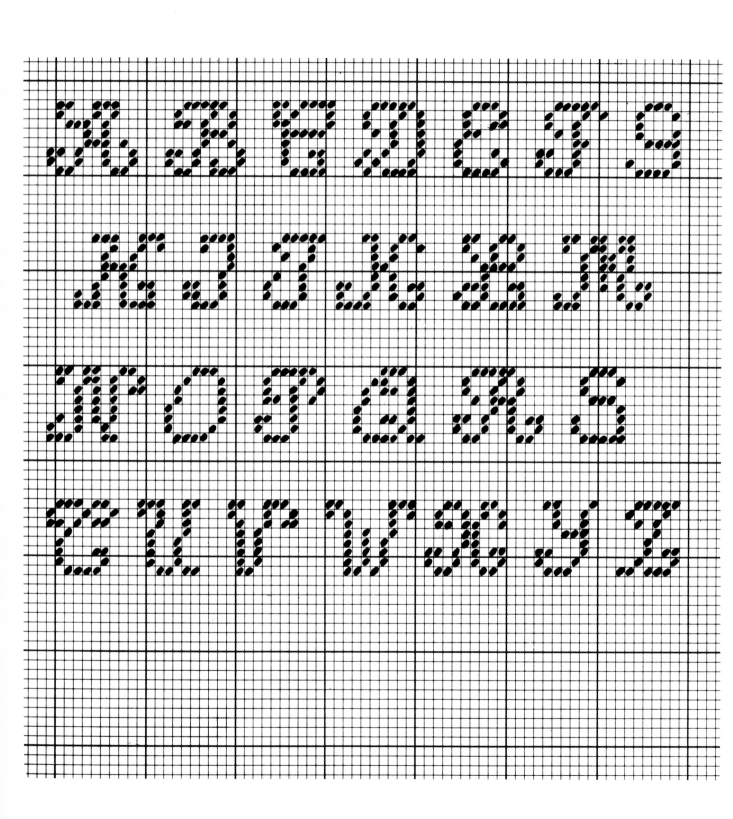

Dieu a créé le monde mais Il a sculpté l'Italie

made before you transfer the design to canvas. And, of course, it is not necessarily the whole design of the pillow or whatsoever you are making that you may want to photostat; you can enlarge just various elements that you will combine into a composition afterwards. Costs of photostats differ all over the country, but it is safe to say that a photostat is cheaper than having a photographic print made of your subject. It is intended to be temporary and is therefore made on inexpensive paper and it will eventually fade. All you have to tell the shop is the overall size of the picture or of the part of the picture you need; tell them to blow it up to six inches or ten inches or whatever you want. Ask for a positive print.

Some photostat shops may not have the facilities for printing a very large stat such as a rug design all in one piece. You can persuade them to blow the design up in sections, all to the same scale, and then tape them together.

If you want to do a repeat of a motif such as the classic stylized fish scale on page 92, for example, you must bear in mind that the motif should repeat often enough so there will be no doubt that it *is* a repeat pattern. Let us say you are working on a fifteen-inch pillow. If you were to plan the fish scale seven-and-a-half inches high, you could repeat only once and this would defeat the purpose. If, on the other hand, you make each fish scale three inches high, you will obtain five repeats, which would be fine. If you make the scale one-and-a-half inches high, you will end up with ten repeats, which admittedly requires more work on a finer canvas. Think this sort of thing out before having photostats made.

I think that, as you become more intrigued with needlepoint, you will not be having your motifs blown up quite so much. You will find that you can get a greater number of smaller interesting shapes into the same area of canvas, using finer and finer mesh sizes on which to render them. The further into this you get, the more you will want to do. Although large flat areas of color make great pillow designs, you will find more intricate ones irresistible as time goes on.

The Outline

Before we go into the method of tracing the design onto paper and canvas, a word about hem allowances. Any piece of needlepoint will have to be turned under around the edges to be mounted, so that when it is attached to the backing fabric the sewing will be done through needlepoint, not just through canvas. Whether you are making a knife-edged or boxed pillow, you will need an extra half inch or three-quarters of an inch of needlepoint all the way around which must be included in the original outline you put on canvas. Then the finished product will be strong enough to take all the pounding and plumping you are bound to give it. The same is true of chair seats and upholstery that are going to be stretched tightly to fit certain contours.

If you are doing needlepoint for a simple chair seat, cover the seat with brown wrapping paper and trace the outline. This becomes the outline on your canvas to which you add a margin for hem. The outline will look much larger than the chair seat because it also takes additional canvas area to cover the rounded or domed shape of the seat. If your needlepoint is to be upholstery for a more complicated chair, bench or stool, ask the upholsterer who will do the final work to make you a paper pattern.

Rug canvas is turned under for hemming right at the last row of needlepoint stitches. No stitches should be turned under at the edges, as the hem would be fat and bulky and would not lie flat.

The Design Onto Tracing Paper

The next step is the tracing of both the outline and the design onto tracing paper.

Tracing paper comes by the roll, generally forty to forty-four inches wide, and in pads of many sizes, in various degrees of transparency. You can always buy tracing paper wider than your canvas, so you can always make the final tracing in one piece. The weight of the paper depends on your design. If there is considerable detail, the paper must allow enough of it to show through, even though you are going to simplify it. But, when I design a rug, for instance, I know I am going to be laying it out on the floor because that is the only area I have big enough to work on. I may kneel on it, walk on it, so my chief requirement for rugs is that the tracing paper be the toughest, and this usually means the thickest.

Now trace the design, or the various elements of the design in progress, from your photostat or other source material. If you are assembling various elements, trace them separately as was described before, then move them about inside the outline you have planned or traced for the project until you have a composition you like. Then trace everything, outline and all, onto one sheet of tracing paper.

Make this final tracing with a black thin-line marking pen. This is important for two reasons: The lines must be black so they will show through clearly when you retrace them onto canvas, and you need a quick-drying marker because pencil or ball-point-pen ink rub off and smear on the slick surface of tracing paper.

If the design has a great many colors, you should outline each area of color on the tracing paper with the black liner. Remember that outlining areas of color is not exactly the same thing as outlining the objects in your design. The areas of different colors within one object, including some of the more strongly contrasting areas in whatever shading there may be, should be outlined, too, to make a clear guide to working the final canvas. But note, also, that this final tracing might not be necessary at all if you happen to be working from a photostat of a previous line drawing or tracing that is fairly simple; you may be able to trace directly onto the canvas from such a photostat.

However you go about doing your tracing, remember that it has two purposes. One is to simplify details in the original, which happens almost automatically because the tracing paper obscures them somewhat. The other is to get everything located where you want it, by trial and error if necessary. You can patch and fix and change as much as you want with pieces of tracing until you have the design you want. Then make a master tracing of the whole thing before you proceed to the canvas. All this preparation is well worth the trouble, for now you don't have to worry about spoiling the more costly canvas by drawing on that by trial and error.

The Color Sketch

There is still one more step you can take before you go on to the canvas, and that is to make a complete color sketch of the whole design. You will have to decide whether or not this is necessary. I usually find that it is not and refer to my original colored source material as I stitch instead. However, if your design seems a little complicated, or if it is assembled from various sources or is composed of elements not originally in color, you may want to test the placement of the colors first.

Over your black tracing put a fresh sheet of good-quality tracing paper and on this paint in the design with acrylic paints. I explain more about these paints further on. They are as easy to use as children's poster paints. With them you can make a color diagram over the line tracing not much more complicated than the filling in of colors in a coloring book that nevertheless gives you a good idea of what your design looks like in full color. Don't be concerned about every detail and gradation of color at this point, as the objective is to "paint" the canvas with the wools later and at your leisure. Presently you should only be plotting the basic color scheme and the placement of colored elements in the composition. However, now you do have a very good guide for transferring the colors to the canvas or to refer to when you are stitching.

The Design Onto Canvas

To see the black master tracing clearly through the canvas, you should first put the tracing on a white surface — a big piece of white paper or even a bed sheet for very large designs. Have your canvas ready: It should be cut an inch or two bigger all around than the overall outline of the final needlepoint, and masking tape should be folded over the cut edges to keep the canvas from fraying. Turn the canvas so that the selvage edge, if any, is at the side, and so that, if you are using double canvas, the "joined" pairs of threads are running up and down in relation to the design.

Lay your canvas on top of the tracing, and you are ready to start transferring the outlines of the design. Before I go into details on how to use the best tools for this, let me say there is no need to tape the canvas to the tracing paper in order to keep it lined up. Nor is there any reason to make an elaborate series of X's or pin marks for "registry" marks. I contend that if you put down the tracing, the canvas on top of it, hold them firmly, and trace one strong shape on the canvas, then that shape becomes your registry mark, that is, your key to lining up the entire design from then on. This works. You can draw one paisley pear, or one flower, or whatever, and if the canvas moves while you are tracing the next pear or flower, simply move the canvas right back so that the key shape is lined up again with the key shape on the tracing. The important advantage of this is that since your canvas is not tacked down, you can lift it up at any point to check that you are getting what you want from the tracing.

Indelible Markers

The best tool to use for tracing the design onto the needlepoint canvas is an indelible marker. The marking pens called Studio Magic Markers are the only ones on the market, as far as I know, that are completely indelible. They are fat little bottles with metal caps and rather broad felt tips, and you will need to trim the tips to a finer point with a razor blade in order to make them render an accurately fine line on the canvas. Despite this slight inconvenience they are the best tool to use in tracing off your design.* Handling, washing, blocking, dry cleaning, nothing will lift the color. This is a necessity, as no color must ever bleed into the yarn. Test any other pen or marker that claims to be waterproof on canvas before using it. I have seen too many pieces of needlepoint laid out with markers that have not been tested for washing and dry cleaning beforehand. Disaster ensues, for when the finished pieces are blocked, the ink runs into the wool and *nothing* can be done to remove it.

You now have several choices for how to proceed with transferring the tracing to the canvas, depending on how complete a replica of the design you want on the canvas before you start to stitch.

You can trace off the whole thing with an indelible marker in only one neutral shade, such as medium gray, and put no color at all on the canvas. If you have a good color original or sketch to use as a guide to filling in with the wool colors, just this outline may be enough, especially for simple designs.

Or, you may need more indication of color on the canvas but may want to avoid something I happen to dislike. This is having so much color painted on the canvas that it actually interferes with your seeing what you are doing when you are working with the wool. The neutral canvas is usually a better background against which to see the progress you are making. I prefer only to outline each area of color in approximately the color with which I intend to fill it in, tracing off the entire black master tracing in the necessary colors. Use your original color source, or a color sketch, or some sort of planned color scheme to refer to as you do this. Currently, Studio Magic Markers come in innumerable colors, offer-

---

* Magic Marker also manufactures "Fine Line" Studio Magic Markers. Some of these have been made to be indelible and some have not. If you can find them, they are ideal, but they *must* be tested for indelibility before using by washing with soap and water.

ing you a wide enough palette for outlining any conceivable design on canvas, but you really need only the basic colors of the overall color scheme, as again this tracing on the canvas is only a guide.

Acrylic Paints

Finally, you may really prefer to work on a painted canvas. First transfer all of the master tracing to the canvas with a gray indelible marker. Then the cleanest, easiest, most sensible way to fill in the colors on the canvas is with acrylic paints, which art-supply stores carry in jars or tubes. These paints are water soluble before they dry, so you can dilute a color and use it as a wash in large areas of your design, or use a color thicker and thinner to indicate shading. You can also mix your own colors instead of taking them as they come. The remarkable thing is that though they are water soluble, once dry the colors are permanent* and the canvas can be washed or dry cleaned and blocked without fear of the paint bleeding through the finished piece of needlepoint. (For years it was customary to use oil paints. They were safe, but much more difficult to handle. You thinned them with turpentine so that you could paint the surface of the canvas without clogging the holes while still keeping them thick enough to maintain their colors. Oil paints are slow to dry, and the smell of turpentine, linseed oil, and paint lingers as long as you work on the canvas.) I do admit that for some people a painted canvas is more reassuring to work on. Acrylic paints give better results than have been possible before.

Remember, nevertheless, that the paint on the canvas need not (in fact, cannot) match the colors of wool exactly nor include every detail and every gradation of shading. It is only another diagram to help you in the stitching. It is even best to keep the paint colors more subdued than the wool colors so the paint will not show through the stitches.

I must warn you, also, to remember to draw the initial outline with a safe color

---

* The formulas for all brands of acrylic paints are not identical. Most are permanent as described here, but you must read the labels to see what is guaranteed in the brand you buy. Those marked "insoluble after drying," as is the Liquitex brand, are safe. A brand marked "water-resistant" should be tested; it may not be water*proof*.

such as gray and not with black as you will see done on some commercial canvases. The black is unnecessary and will certainly show through under pale colors. Some people even make the mistake of literally following those dark outlines in wool before filling in with color, and the result tags the effort as very amateurish. Unless the yellow daisies you are working are designed to be outlined in black wool, do not draw them on the canvas in black.

While we are on the subject of black, it is murder to work black yarn on black-painted canvas. I use a gray paint or marker instead on the canvases I design, and I direct people to fill in anything of that gray with black yarn. It is much easier. Furthermore, when a design calls for black yarn, I find a softer brown black more appealing than pitch black.

Color

People have written learned books on the subject of color, and I am no authority. But I have my own ideas, and so, I hope, will you, if not at first, eventually. I pick colors that please me. If I am designing a piece of needlepoint for a particular room, I am naturally conscious of choosing colors that will go into that room, perhaps repeating colors in the curtain or upholstery. Suppose you have a slipcover print of many shades of green, with white and perhaps yellow, and just a few touches of red. It would make sense to do the pillow with a hot red background not only to pick up the touches of red in the fabric but also to attract attention to the pillow. When you go to the trouble of making a piece of needlepoint, I think the eye should be drawn to it when one enters the room. I have seen people wait for their friends to respond to a new needlepoint pillow they have put their blood into be so disappointed when nobody noticed it. The pillow just melted into the room instead of having been treated as something to be noticed. The classic "safe" colors of the past, black and maroon and beige, are no longer popular. Put some real color into your needlepoint. You will find that today we all live with color more easily than we used to. And to me, needlepoint is an ideal place to exaggerate color because it is necessarily confined to a small area. You might willingly buy a painting in wonderful wild colors, frame it, and hang it on a wall as a focal point in a room. Why not a needlepoint pillow or rug or whatever?

People who are scared of color get over it. As they become accustomed to doing needlepoint, it seems to me their choice of color gets bolder, even in the simplest projects. A friend of mine started working on squares of needlepoint all with the identical butterfly motif but in assorted color combinations. He had no idea what he intended to use them for. He picked up several canvas and yarn kits of these butterfly designs and worked the brown and yellow one first, then another with several shades of blue and black and white. Now he says he is doing butterflies in hot pinks and orange and white, and in brilliant purple with a little bit of green and black and white. He must be up to number twenty-three at least. The more he does, the wilder the colors get and the more he loves them. He does not know where it is all going to end. The project began as a patchwork pillow with nine squares, then with sixteen, then with twenty. He may end up with upholstery in butterflies.

I pick colors by seeing the wool and handling it. The colors must please me in the hand if they are ever to please me on canvas. But you can count on the fact that, however brilliant the yarn may look in the skein, you will lose some of the intensity of the color from the time you thread the needle to the time it has been stitched down. This has to do with a different reflection of light when the yarn has been pulled tight on a flat surface.

The only bits of bookishness I want to impart to you are some elementary notions of how basic types of color affect each other.

Complementary colors, for instance. If you put red beside green, the green will look greener and the red will look redder. Any two complementary colors will make each other stronger; orange and blue or yellow and purple together will behave just like red and green. To put this into practice, if you are doing a design that is predominantly green, a red background will make the greens look green as hell.

Value, or the lightness and darkness of colors, gives clarity to a design. For a first project, for instance, it is generally a good idea to limit the number of colors. You might choose two colors each of a different value plus a light (probably white) and a dark. If you are planning a blue and green pillow and both colors are of equal value, they will have the effect of a single color. This might be offset by having larger areas of one than of the other in the design. But if the colors are of different values and are used in different quantities as well, the result will be definitely more interesting.

Neutral colors and strong colors work interestingly together. This is a contrast of intensities. If I am working a central motif that is subtle, maybe in a range of grays or browns, I automatically choose the hottest, wildest color possible for the background. It is amazing to discover how the two never kill each other; what has been done in great detail in petit point in neutral colors holds its own against any kind of violent background. By the same token, a sun face in brilliant high-noon shades of orange, yellow and red will look best against a pale, bleached-out sky blue — which also happens to be the kind of a sky a brilliant hot sun is usually in.

There are occasions when you want to force colors to work against each other for effect — in "op" designs, for instance. Strong colors all of the same intensity will "bounce." If you hold two handfuls of wool together and have to say, "They hurt my eyes," they are fighting each other, or bouncing. Of course, the design will hold up under this onslaught only if the bounce between the shapes of color is intentional.

You should play with wool colors in the skein at first, to see how these things work and to select the colors you like, just as you play with the elements of the design in preliminary tracings.

Shading and Modeling

You need not start with designs that require shading or realistic modeling, but you may soon want to try. What you do is select your basic color scheme, and then select gradations of the colors. You can limit the number of gradations, but even if you are just learning it is not necessary to confine yourself merely to two or three.

Suppose you are shading a flower petal from the center of the flower to the end of the petal, and you know that what you are copying starts dark at the edge of the petal and gets very light toward the center, as happens in so many flowers. It is no more problem to break up this petal into five areas of graduated color than it is to break it up into three. For that matter, why not break it up into nine areas? What is important is that no two petals of the flower should be broken up the same way; the sizes and numbers of areas should vary. Irregularity is desirable in needlepoint. This is what gives life to the finished piece. You can fuss with as many shades or gradations of any one color as you are lucky enough to lay your hands on and can put your mind to using as long as you do not handle them repetitively. You will learn that the more shading you put into an object, the more depth, the more punch, the more realism it will appear to have, if that is the objective of the kind of design you are doing. On the other hand, if you set out to do an all-over pattern of, say, twenty stylized flowers, each in a different color to make a series of bright splotches against the background, subtle shading of the flower heads will just weaken them and kill the design. In any case, if you don't want to get into too complicated shading, Pasternayan wool simplifies your choice of colors because there are no more than five shades of any one of them. If you want to go further, you can split the yarns as is explained below.

The so-called blur in needlepoint caused by working colors of nearly the same value and intensity close together in a design can sometimes be highly desirable. Suppose you have designed a floral pattern with a background color close to some of the colors in the flowers. If a flower melts into the background at some point where it goes darker or lighter, the effect will only heighten the modeling at some other point where the colors lift the flower away from the background. The blur in one place helps to throw the flower as a whole into relief.

I have sometimes been asked just "how" one does shading and modeling. There is no exact "how" that can be described to you because every motif you might shade is different from the next. In your mind's eye it can be compared to the same process in painting. But since you are using wool stitches, you can tell "how" best by experimenting with the specific group of graduated colors you want to use. A trial leaf on a scrap of canvas will tell you more about the effect you can get from placing little areas of wool tones next to each other in graduated sequences than any directions you can read. I would recommend making the trial scrap of canvas at least large enough to make a coaster or some small object, as it may turn out well on the first try.

Splitting Wool Colors

If you are limited in the number of shades of wool colors you can get, you can split apart the threads or plies of your yarns and combine plies of different shades of the same color. In a background or solid area, this gives a tweedy, textured look.

If you are trying to model a subject, get some roundness into a motif, you can increase your range of colors by splitting. Suppose you have black, dark gray, medium gray, light gray, and white. You can take a ply of white and one of light gray and combine them; then a ply of light gray and one of medium gray; a ply of medium gray and one of dark gray; a ply of dark gray and one of black. With these combinations, you end up with nine gradations instead of the original five. In most circumstances, I am more likely to mix together colors I already have to get more variations for a motif than I am to go out and buy more colors of yarn.

The Background

In general, do not be trapped into doing something dull by trying to play safe with colors. Nevertheless, as I mentioned earlier, you might take some precautions such as not choosing a background color until the design is finished. This is often what I do with projects of my own. Sometimes for a complicated motif with many colors or a great deal of shading, the design has to be finished before I can decide on a background color that can fight it out with the design and hold its own. Other times, the shading may be so subtle that the design may turn out to need an especially strong background color to set it off.

I have known many people to start big projects, such as rugs with a lot of design on them, and, because they did not know and how long it would take to complete the rug, to hold off buying yarn for the background. They might not, after all, be living in the same house by the time they got around to the background or might not want to use the rug in the same room it was originally intended for. So it can be best to postpone the choice of background to see where the rug will finally be used. In the meantime, it is not a bad idea to put in a small square of a proposed background color to learn to live with it while you work the central motif. If the color turns out to be less than you hoped for, you can easily take out the square and substitute another color altogether for the final background.

*Detail of robin's-nest footstool
in color picture 11*

4 Six Seat Cushions

A set of four Sheraton ballroom chairs, a Sheraton rocker, and a Sheraton footstool became a multiple project in my apartment. As I said before, I see no reason for seat cushions to match. To me, six all alike would not only be dull to do but dull to live with afterwards. The bond in common for these is the backing material and the basic shape. The subjects are all completely different and come from completely different sources — almost a summary of the kinds of design sources proposed throughout this book, such as art books, magazine illustrations, photography, old engravings, plus a collection of "favorite things" and a simple original sketch.

The head of the ram in color picture 6 is my favorite, taken from an old German engraving in the library. It is drawn naturalistically, with marvelous decorations of green grape leaves, red ribbon, and a golden bell. The original was black and white, of course, and I did the needlepoint in the most logical colors. When the ram was done, in petit point, the only color missing was blue. Since he is clearly looking for trouble ahead, I began the background, in gros point, with the lightest blues in the direction of his glare and deepened them gradually across the pillow like a rainbow.

In color picture 7 is an undersea series of crabs, sponges, coral, rock, and sand in natural colors against a sandy yellow ground. Its inspiration was an illustration by Rudolph Freund for a nature series in *Life* Magazine. This particular grouping was lifted by photostat out of one corner of the painting and edited to eliminate everything behind the two crabs. The sand floor beyond holds the elements together. Because of the detail, this was all done in petit point.

The composition in color picture 8 is not mine but photographer Horst's, representing the plaster casts that art students use to learn to sketch heads, arms, figures. The casts were done in petit point, modeled in grays like the photograph. The background is stitched in gros point in shades of beige that drift across the canvas diagonally in waves to relieve the starkness of the composition.

The origin of the design in color picture 9 is a detail of Michelangelo's design for a column capital in St. Peter's. I found it in the library and had just the medallion statted to size. It is worked in muddy yellows and browns against a bright yellow background. This was an exercise in modeling, too, but the shape is bold and did not require petit point.

The chair seat in color picture 10 is a collection of favorite things, each item worked by itself in petit point with its own gros-point background. They are a butterfly, mushroom, jack-in-the-pulpit, crystal, chambered nautilus, humming-bird, holly, chipmunk, and tree frog. To tie them all together I worked a tiny Greek-key braid interlocking the squares.

The cosy nest of three blue robin's eggs I designed myself for the Sheraton footstool in color picture 11. The prospect of putting one's feet on a nest filled with eggs I thought was an irresistible needlepoint joke. I sketched this from a bird's nest I contrived myself, a ring of fried Chinese noodles. The black-and-white detail on page 72 shows how the strands are made to look laced together, over and under each other. The roundness of nest and eggs was too symmetrical, so I added the feather.

For these seat cushions, as with the majority of pieces I have done in both petit point and gros point, I used No. 12/24 double canvas which unfortunately is not consistently available. You can get it, however (see Shopping Information on page 183). For some though not all designs, I like it better than the more common 10/20 canvas because the background gros-point stitch is not too coarse in relation to the petit-point stitch. Once you make up your mind you like doing petit point, the best thing is to lay in a supply of several yards. You may not be able to get it immediately, but if you have enough to take care of projects for a year or two ahead, you can spare yourself the inconvenience of trying to buy small pieces over and over again, and maybe by the time you run out it will be easier to get.

The backing of all these pillows was originally black silk faille. When they began to look worn around the edges, I had them taken apart, cleaned, reblocked, and rebacked with lightweight wool that has outworn the silk but will certainly not outwear the needlepoint.

5 *Compositions Entirely Your Own*

The idea of choosing your own themes for subject matter can be extended to designs altogether different from the "favorite-things" seat cushion in color picture 10. Pets, for instance. Portraits of pets, unfortunately, remind me of bronzed baby shoes. The final object should be, but seldom is, pleasing to look at. What seems to be missing is the element of design. I avoid portraits of pets for this reason, but a friend asked me to lay out a pillow of her Yorkshire and I said I would try. I know this Yorkshire well, a tiny monster that is a frequent house-guest of mine. The more I looked at her, the more impossible it seemed. This portrait was surely going to look like one of those kits you send away for.

When the Yorkshire stays with me, she curls up next to whatever chair I am sitting in. Looking down at her one evening, I realized that this curled-up creature was not so much a Yorkshire terrier with a face as just some marvelous kind of shape. The more I thought about it, the more attractive she was from this angle.

For her pillow in color picture 3, I sketched the dog myself when she was asleep and she came out more characteristically herself than any portrait. If you aren't up to drawing your pet, take a photograph of him to work from instead. I'm sure he will be more beguiling asleep like this than in any conventional pose. I decided the pillow might as well be useful in the bargain, so it is just of a size for the Yorkshire to curl up on herself. The dog is salt-and-pepper colored, the head black with blond streaks. White highlights on the black nose make it look shiny and alive. To indicate indentations made on the pillow by the needlepoint dog, I added very simple black and gray lines radiating from the rump, which is usually the heaviest part of a dog. To break up the background, I stitched a fake tassel at the left and sewed a real one on the other side.

Photostats of pictures of individual objects made the curious assemblage in color picture 12. The stats were shuffled until the arrangement pleased me, with some of the objects placed as if they were on a shelf (silver urn and bowl, which are Greek pieces, Egyptian scarab, eye of Horus, snake coiled around an egg) and others flat against the wall above (ribbon twisted into a monogram "L," my first piece of needlepoint caning, medallion with gems, and, "pinned" on the background through a key, a monogram "G" in the shape of a hydra that looks as if it were on a page torn from a book).

The shadows give depth to the objects, but actually the shading is limited because I did the design in silk petit point (on single canvas) and silk does not

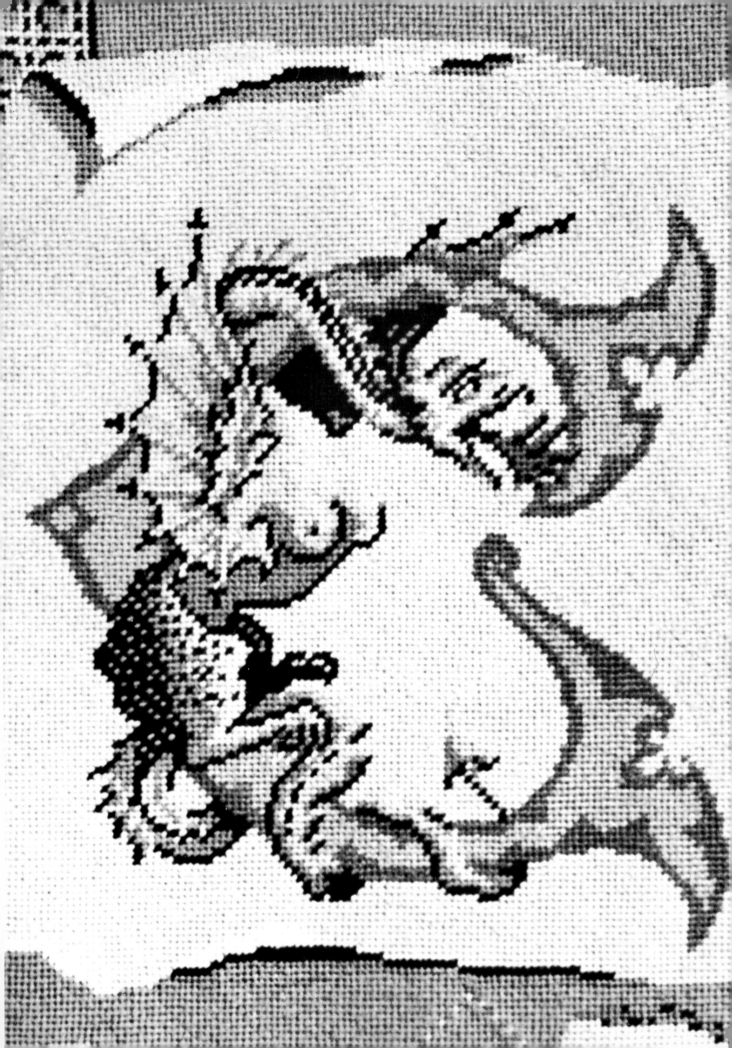

come in a very wide range of colors. However, silk is very good for detail and for rendering metallic objects because of its own natural sheen. The best silks are French, good hard silks that are tightly twisted. They are expensive and for this reason hard to come by because of the sizeable investment for the importer.

A fool-the-eye shadow box is a good background for composing an arrangement of favorite objects. The one in color picture 13 finally did contain a small portrait of "Herself" the Yorkshire, and an anemone, smoky topaz crystals, and seashells, all of which are favorite things of my friend, the dog's owner. I drew this composition, but you could cut out pictures of objects and compose them as I did in the preceding silk picture. The shadow box is not hard to plot yourself. Or you could work with real objects, place them in a box, rig a strong light to cast shadows, and take a photograph of the arrangement. Have it photostated to the size you want. Instead of framing this design, I had it mounted on a block of wood so that it could stand and become an object.

There is another shadow-box arrangement in color picture 33.

Detail from color picture 12

6 Repeat Patterns

The repertory of fifty-four repeat patterns I have worked out in the patchwork samplers (color pictures 19 and 21) do not have to be painted nor even drawn on the canvas to be worked. They are made up of no more than three to five colors and you count out, right from the printed page, the number and placement of the stitches on blank canvas. (Granted, for the designs shown in petit point, a magnifying glass helps, but when you have worked a motif on canvas once, you use this as the guide for repeating.) You can work them all on any mesh size of canvas, from petit-point to rug canvas, and you can invent any color scheme you want for them. The designs range in style from traditional motifs such as the fleur-de-lys, Greek key, or paisley to throbbing "op"-work checkerboards to brickwork, chicken wire, caning, or basketry. It is surprising how easily the three-dimensional quality of some of them is rendered in the two dimensions of needlepoint canvas.

How to Use Repeat Patterns

Any one of the designs could be repeated as an all-over pattern to cover a pillow, make upholstery for a chair seat or bench, or make a rug. But they are far more versatile than that. They can be used as mini-designs to make up into coasters for glasses. (Do each square on a small piece of canvas. Leave a half-inch margin of blank canvas all the way around, snip it carefully at the corners, fold it under, and paste the needlepoint onto a backing of felt with any of the white glues such as Sobo or Elmer's. Once the white glue has set, the pieces will not separate even if the glue gets damp. Being made of wool, the coasters will absorb water, dry completely, and perform indefinitely.) Any of the designs that repeat either vertically or horizontally, rather than on the diagonal — in other words, one with a striped quality — can become a border for a pillow or rug. The same designs would do well as straps for a luggage rack (and with a glass top on it, the luggage rack might do well as a coffee table), or for tapes to trim window valances, curtain headings, or the frame of a tester bed.

Slippers or scuffs for a man or a woman in any of the repeat designs make impressive gifts. The amount of needlepoint is minimal, though the cost of having your needlepoint made up into slippers may be something else again. Find yourself a good shoemaker first and establish a price. Needlepoint scuffs are luxurious and

*Men's scuffs covered, left to right, in trompe-
l'oeil grid, "Op" blocks, outlined Swedish crosses,
a simple basketry motif, and needlepoint caning.*

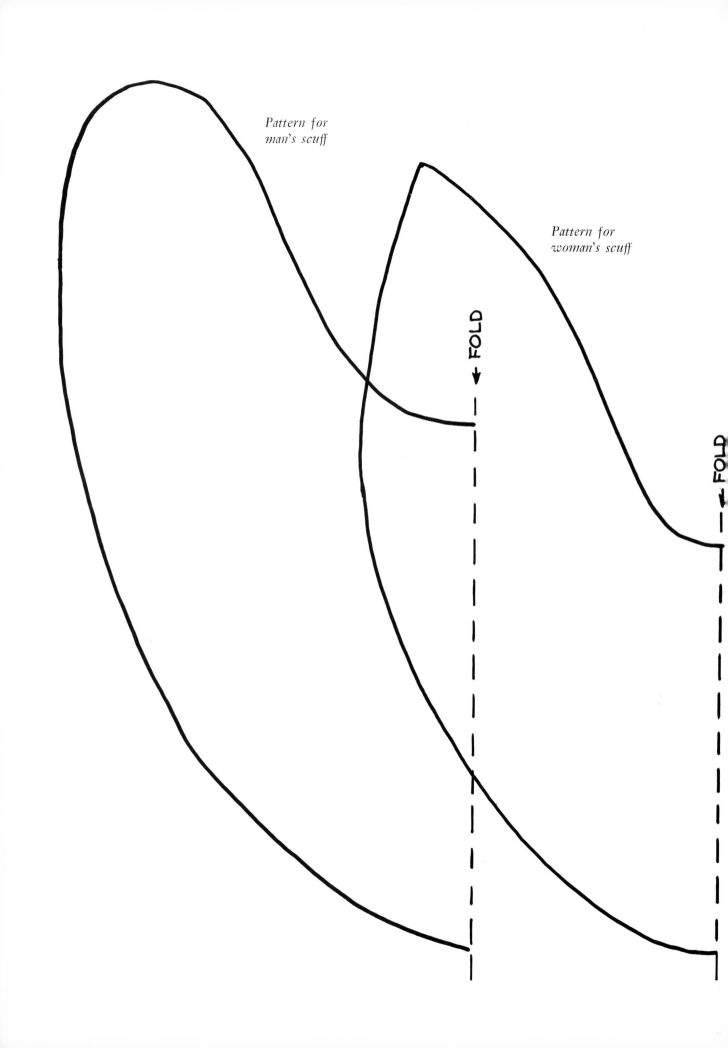

Pattern for
man's scuff

Pattern for
woman's scuff

FOLD

FOLD

should be leather lined. The two patterns provided opposite fit any man or any woman because there is no heel to be sized. If you want to make closed slippers, have the shoemaker draw you the pattern for the necessary shoe size.

Still another use for repeat patterns, especially the more bold "Op" variety, is to cover a brick doorstop. The pattern for the canvas is on page 82, with dimensions to fit a standard construction brick. But, find your brick first and adapt the pattern to it if necessary. Draw the pattern on an oblong of canvas, and, unless you are good at this sort of thing, have it mounted on a brick for you by a needlepoint shop. The cost will be less by far than having slippers made. However, the general idea is, after you have sewn up the corners of the needlepoint to make the brick shape, to trim the canvas not too close to the needlepoint, put in the brick, and glue the excess canvas to the bottom of the brick. Then glue a piece of leather or felt to the bottom of the brick.

Of course, there is no reason to limit yourself to repeat patterns for either slippers or bricks. Leopard spots (page 109) or fool-the-eye malachite (page 105) or marble (page 100), or any design you would use for pillows or anything else is possible as long as the design fits the rather small space.

One of the most fascinating ways to use repeat patterns is for backgrounds for central motifs instead of the usual solid backgrounds. For example, if your central design on a rug or pillow were an armful of tulips, you could work out a basketry pattern for the background (for a large version, see page 94). For many subjects you can find some such logical motif to stitch around them that will add a great deal to the finished work and will be a big relief if doing plain backgrounds bores you. Or, conversely, one classic way to design a rug is to make an elaborate border of large scale, such as the acanthus-leaf border on page 169, and to leave the center area plain or at least uniform. I couldn't make myself do that much plain stitching, but filling the center area with one of the bolder geometric patterns such as the "Op" blocks, octagon tiling, or Swedish crosses makes an excellent texture inside the bold frame.

In stitching a repeat pattern, you will usually want to finish a two-to-four-inch patch of it with all the colors to see what it looks like before covering a large area with it. You can continue with one color at a time or finish small patches completely one after the next as you prefer or as seems most practical for counting out the particular pattern. There is one design, the caning pattern, for which it is best to use a systematic method to cover large areas. The instructions are given below. But for this one, too, you need to finish a small patch to be sure the colors you have chosen do give the intended trompe-l'oeil effect.

How to Do Cane-pattern Needlepoint

The ovals represent stitches in four different colors: clear for light yellow, deep gray for medium yellow, black for black, and light gray for the background color, which should be a bright shade of red, green, or blue to make the caning stand out. The cane grids should be executed first in light yellow. These are the parallel rows of stitches that run horizontally and vertically on the canvas and serve as a framework for the rest of the stitchery.

In a horizontal direction from right to left along the top edge of your canvas,

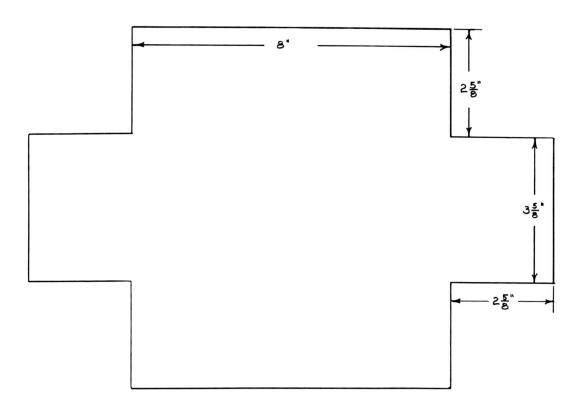

Light yellow

Medium yellow

Black

Bright background color

Opposite, needlepoint pattern for brick doorstop.
Measure out the pattern on an oblong of canvas,
and do not trim the canvas until it is ready to be
mounted. If you mount it yourself, it is a good
idea to machine-stitch a narrow tape to the edge
of the canvas after you trim it, to avoid fraying
while you "upholster" the brick.

84

work two light-yellow rows in the Continental stitch, skipping one row between. Count down five spaces in the canvas and, beginning in the sixth, work two more rows, skipping a row between. Continue to the bottom edge of the canvas.

Return to the upper right-hand corner of your canvas and work a vertical row of light-yellow stitches to the bottom edge of the canvas. Skip one row to the left and work a second row parallel to your first. Skip five rows and repeat the pair of vertical rows, continuing in this fashion to the left-hand edge of the canvas.

In medium-yellow yarn, follow the pattern laid out on the diagram in deep gray. These rows should be worked diagonally. Count over four stitches from the top right-hand corner of your grid and then count down four stitches. Take your first stitch (this stitch will fall in the upper right corner of the little square formed by the grid), and proceed to work in a diagonal line, skipping three spaces or stitches each time. Continue to the lower left corner of your canvas. For the parallel diagonal, count over six stitches from the top right-hand corner of your grid, and down one stitch. Working in a diagonal line parallel to the previous row of stitches, fill in the empty spaces, which will be every other stitch. Repeat this pattern of diagonal rows toward the left-hand edge of the canvas. Your series of rows will all fall in the upper left triangular half of your canvas. You then make similar parallel rows of medium-yellow stitches across the right half, starting parallel to the central diagonal line and finishing up in the lower right-hand corner of the canvas.

Next, thread your needle with the black yarn which will serve as shadow. Work first horizontally, filling the empty spaces in the rows you skipped between

19

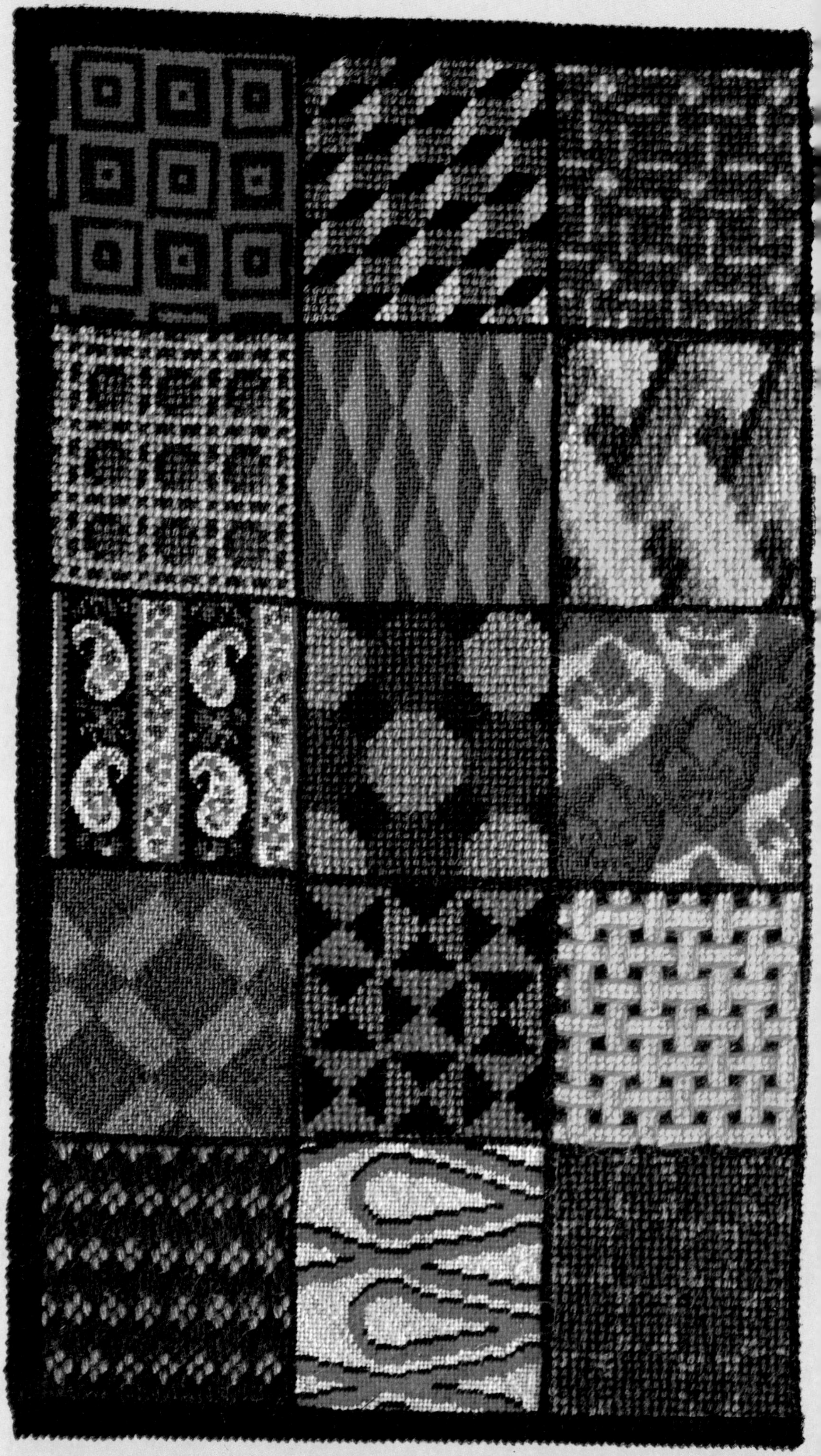

the pairs of light-yellow horizontal stitches that form the grid. Then, fill in the empty spaces in the rows between the vertical parallel rows of light-yellow stitches.

Now you are ready to fill in the squares formed by the grid. Start with the square at the top right-hand corner of your canvas. At this point, it should be defined by a solid row of light yellow, and each of the inside corners should be punctuated by one stitch in medium yellow. Work your black yarn in the following way: Take one stitch below the top right corner stitch inside the square, three stitches to fill in the top row, three more stitches to fill in the left-hand side, then one stitch to the right of the medium-yellow stitch in the bottom left corner. Repeat until all the squares in one vertical row are done. Then return to the top of your canvas and do all the squares in the next vertical row, and so on.

Last comes filling in the centers of the squares, which you do in the basket-weave stitch in the bright background color. Again, fill in the squares in one vertical row at the right-hand edge of your canvas, and continue in vertical rows to the left-hand edge of the canvas.

Four-way Repeats

Paper cutouts are another way to achieve repeat patterns, and they make handsome formal designs of the simplest basic motifs. They work on the same principle as many tile designs. The four corners of the design are identical, and the two sides of the initial motif are also identical on either side of a diagonal center line, so that however you turn the final design it is always symmetrical.

You can look for motifs to copy, among tile designs especially, but it's no trick at all to make your own. Fold a square of paper of the size you want to work with in four, making a smaller square. Then fold this diagonally, so that the previously folded edges of the square are on top of each other. Draw a simple design on the resulting triangle, and cut the design out. When you open the diagonal fold, you will have a diagonally symmetrical motif, as in the sketch. When you open the whole square, you will have a four-way repeat of the motif. Trace it first onto tracing paper and then onto canvas. (After the first of the four quarters has been worked, the remaining sets are counted out rather than drawn on the canvas if you wish the repeats to be *exact* duplicates of the first.)

Large-scale Repeats

Many of the patterns on the two samplers can be adapted to a much larger scale and, if they are not too specifically geometrical, they can be traced on the canvas rather than counted out stitch by stitch. Some examples, which would make good rug backgrounds or very bold pillows, are the classic fish-scale pattern, open basketry or laced polls, and bamboo trellis on pages 92-94. Blown up by photostat to approximately the dimensions given, such large repeats can be stitched effectively with little or no counting.

An easy change in scale was used in the seat cushions in color picture 18. The designs are shown in petit point in the sampler in color picture 19 and were simply copied on No. 14 canvas for the cushions, which made the patterns about four times as large. In the cushion on the left are windmills, on the right, squared circles. The thing that was the most fun about these is that they were stitched entirely with wool colors left over from other projects.

One quarter of paper cutout for four-way repeat

Above, classic fish-scale pattern. Photostat ten inches wide or more, or redraw yourself with semicircles two and a half inches or more in diameter. The motif can be endlessly repeated. Use any color scheme you choose, as fish scales, even real ones rather than imaginary ones such as these, are every imaginable color in nature. Each row of scales can be done in a different solid color, like the three-tone miniature version in the sampler in color picture 21. Or, each scale can be shaded from dark at the base to pure white at the outer curve, with the white put in as a rippled edge as shown on three scales of the tracing.

Opposite, bamboo trellis. Photostat up to eighteen inches high for a rug background. The pattern can be repeated over as large an area as you want. Draw grooves in the bamboo so that they vary from one section to the next. For a three-dimensional effect, shadows may be indicated on the background, and the side of the bamboo away from the shadow can be highlighted by stitching in a lighter color than the rest. Strong seminaturalistic colors are good for this, against a bright background—the same principle as the yellows against bright color used in needlepoint caning (page 83). Try tones of yellow with brown streaks for the bamboo and perhaps a strong Bristol-blue background with very dark brown-black shadows.

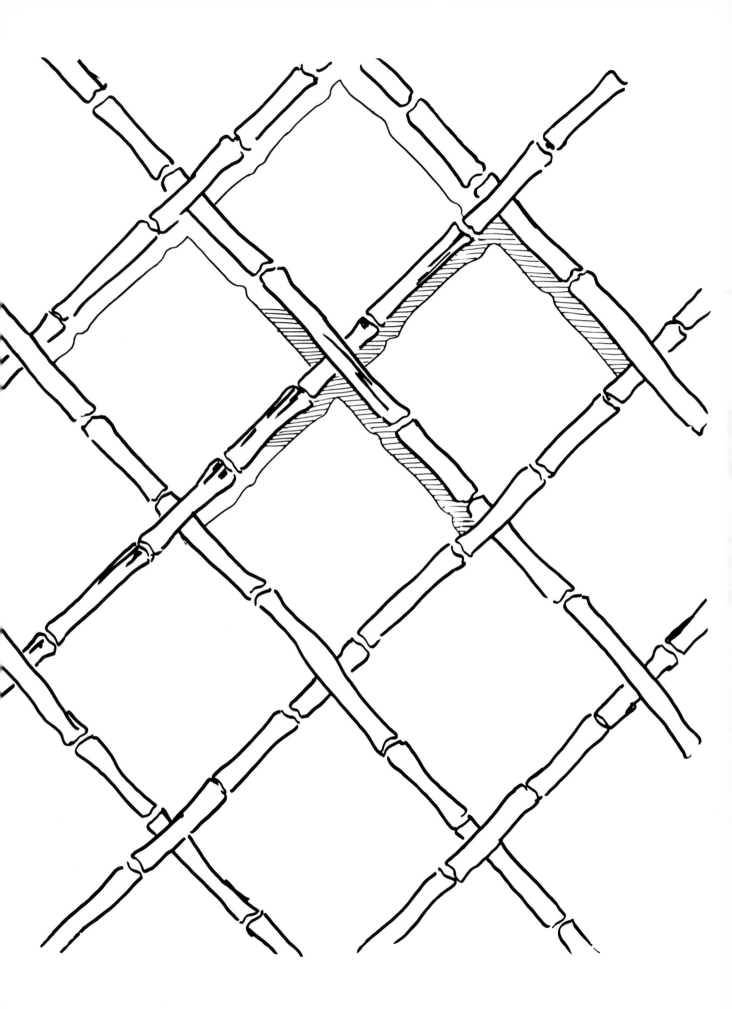

Open basketry or laced polls. Photostat to at least fifteen inches wide for a pillow (repeat to fill pillow square), or enlarge as much more as you wish for a rug background. Again, more or less naturalistic colors are the most convincing—yellows, tans, or muted greens for the basketry, against a very strong background. Three colors laid on without shading—one for the verticals and two alternating for the cross-weaving—will render the woven effect. However, you can also shade the cross-weaving, darkest at the points that go "under" the vertical polls, lightest at the centers of the curves where they go "over." The polls, too, could be shaded to make them round, dark at the sides, light in the middle. But this can get confusing and the effect is likely to be stronger if the polls are left one flat color as the natural rushes in this kind of weaving often are.

7 Fool-the-eye Patterns

Fool-the-eye patterns taken from nature are very different from geometric fool-the-eye repeat patterns. They are much freer and, in fact, it would be better to give them different names — the French names for *faux* (false or fake) designs that are the traditional terms used in interior decoration. *Faux marbre* (marbleizing) and *faux bois* (wood graining) have been in use for centuries as painted finishes. They translate beautifully into needlepoint. Needlepoint malachite is a particular passion of mine. And recently I did a fake tortoise-shell pillow for Isabel O'Neil.

Tortoise Shell

Mrs. O'Neil's fabulous *faux* finishes on painted furniture had long inspired me and I had just finished one of her *faux* tortoise-shell pieces. The needlepoint *faux* tortoise in color picture 22 is a "double" fake, having been done with the colors of the painted piece in mind, and it has ended up nicknamed the "*faux faux*" tortoise.

The tortoise on the pillow is not meant to be realistic and the shape has been simplified. I found a tiny black-and-white picture of a real tortoise in the Sunday *New York Times* and from the photostat traced only the main outline and the shapes of the scales of the shell. A palette of six tortoise colors, including deep browns, pale beige, off-white, and medium caramel brown, is required. Each scale or piece of the shell should be as different as possible from the others. If you study a real piece of tortoise shell, you will see the subtle variations that nature provides. You can't go far wrong if you refer to a real source.

But, in complete departure from realism in this animal, I ran the cathedral red of the background into the seams between the scales of the tortoise shell. Once the tortoise colors had been worked, I could see the design needed some kind of kick, and amazingly, brilliant as this red is, it ties the tortoise scales and the whole design together. Traditionally, tortoise shell has been used as a framing motif, so I made a fanciful frame of tortoise scales, floating them around the red background which became much more interesting to work than a blank expanse of red.

As backing material for the pillow, I chose wide-wale red corduroy, as I could not turn up the right red in either velvet or silk. Some people were horrified at my putting so much work into a piece of needlepoint and then backing it with

21. Patchwork sampler repeat patterns (page 78)
Turn the book so that the righthand side
of the page is at the top.

SQUARES, ROW BY ROW:
Diagonal key, Waffle, Portuguese basketry,
Oriental interlocking ribbon, Brickwork

Op checkerboard, Outlined Swedish crosses,
Open basketry or laced polls,
Topiary trees, Plaid

Hound's-tooth check, Kindergarten, Latticework,
Chicken wire, Fish scales

BORDERS AT FAR RIGHT, TOP TO BOTTOM:
Twisted rope, Braided rope,
Conventional checkerboard, Mini checkerboard,
Simple Greek key, Proper Greek key,
Tiny braid edging, Whitecaps, String of pearls

just plain cotton corduroy. But it looks very well and it's tough, which means it will last a while. Needlepoint will outwear the stoutest fabric, as I have said before, and even the corduroy will have to be replaced eventually. But there is no reason why backing should not be replaced occasionally. As to what is an appropriate backing, with the right design even ordinary cotton ticking could make an excellent and durable backing.

Marble

Once you have traced and stitched a marble pattern, you will see that it is such a free and hazy design that you can easily sketch and extend your own free hand to cover any area you want. A marble-top table or a piece of marbleized paper are sources easy to come by. The sketch on page 100 is convenient, however, because it is bolder and easier to see for tracing than some real marbles. To work marble on No. 10 rug canvas, have the sketch photostated to about eighteen inches high; for No. 14 canvas for a pillow, you could trace the sketch directly from the printed page.

The positive print of a stat will give you this grey-and-white marble with black lines; the negative will give you a guide to black and dark-grey marble with white lines. Trace directly from the stat onto canvas, but, rather than outline the tones as you would normally do for more definite patterns, roughly fill in the areas of each tone. Use blunt, felt-tipped indelible Studio Magic Markers (page 65) in two tones of medium grey and one dark grey or black. (Even if you are doing black marble, do not use very dark markers or you will not be able to see what you are doing when you stitch.) There is no need to be exact when you trace marble nor when you stitch it. On the contrary, it must be irregular.

21

Needlepoint marble tones need to be somewhat more contrasting than in the real thing in order for the effect to come off. Real marbles are varied in color as well as pattern, of course. Combinations of wool tones for several marble colors are given with the multicolored inlaid-marble rug pattern on page 167.

Wood Grain

In color picture 23 is the only copy of a painting I have ever tried to make, and it is not really a copy as I never saw the original. My source was a black-and-white photograph of the painting, by Paul Cadmus. It appealed to me because of the many textures in the various elements, and I made up my own colors. The driftwood, wood grain of the wall, seashells, feathers, bones, each of these was a project in itself. The hands of the young man holding the mobile presented a double challenge. The drawing is intricate and at the time I did not have access to a great range of colors, so I had to work out the modeling with a few colors by breaking up the forms into planes.

I had the photograph blown up, made a careful tracing, and transferred this to canvas. My plan was to do the mobile in petit point and all the rest in gros point. But then I realized the figure would look wrong in gros point behind the finely detailed mobile and would have to be done in petit point. Before long I knew I was trapped, and this is why I am not going to get into a facsimile of a painting again. The background of fine wall-to-wall wood grain would look mushy in gros point. The entire canvas had to be done in the small stitch, and I estimate it took about three-quarters of a million stitches to finish it. I got tired of doing wood grain but otherwise was fascinated. The finished piece was too big for a pillow and unsuitable for any piece of furniture I had, so I had it framed and hung it like a painting.

Closer to life size, wood grain does not by any means have to be done in petit point. The tracing on page 102 can be used directly from the printed page for a fine grain, but blown up to eighteen inches high it will give you the scale of life-sized plywood which could be done in quite a coarse stitch. The possibilities are endless for patterns, size, and colors of wood grain. You can trace samples easily from floors, furniture, and wallpapers, though once you have studied a wood grain it is just about as easy to sketch it freehand. On page 103, details from

*Marble. This can be used any size, but the smaller
the pattern, the finer your canvas should be.
Blown up to about eighteen inches high the design
will be in good scale for a rug design (page 167).*

101

the "painting" show what needlepoint wood grains look like close to, and the color picture of it is a pretty extensive source in itself for variations of color and grain.

Malachite

When real malachite is used to make boxes, trays, obelisks and so on, it is sliced into pieces and fitted together like veneer. The small box in color picture 2 (frontispiece) is made this way. Under the glass on the table in the same picture is my malachite rug which is shown again in color picture 24. The rug is a reasonable though much enlarged facsimile of the top of the little box, made of eleven pieces of veneered malachite. The straight lines that cut through the flowing malachite pattern are the cut edges of the fitted pieces. Is it any wonder that this was one of my pet projects? Although the design has a disciplined shape, there is no rule about putting one shade of green next to the other, as long as it is a good malachite color, and no rule to prevent you from making lines wider or narrower to suit yourself as the patterns grow on your canvas.

Another reason this project enchanted me was that for the first time I was able to find true malachite-green colors in a new line of yarns imported by the Nantucket Needleworks (Shopping Information on page 183). A malachite design can be done with Paternayan wools, but the available colors are not true to life. But I added other colors too. One very muted green made all the other sharp greens look more so, as did a soft brown-black and pure white, which are not malachite colors. The reason for the extra colors is to keep the drama of contrast in the original malachite when the pattern is blown up much larger than life. Both the black and the white make the greens look greener, and the white works in effect like a highlight, the gleam on the surface of polished malachite.

I made the malachite pillow shown on page 106 and in the frontispiece before I made the rug to see if this untried design would work well. (I don't know why I worried.) Certainly a pillow is a good idea if the thought of a large rug intimidates you. Both the pillow and the rug were worked in the same way, one section of the veneer at a time, with the same colors. I started at the top right-hand corner and counted the sections as I went along. It's a satisfying way to work. By the time four sections of the pillow are done, it is half complete, and

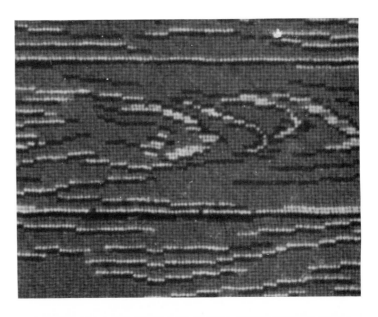

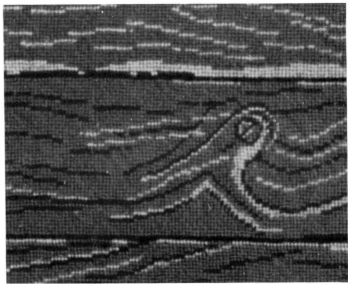

Left, wood grain. This can be traced as is on No. 14 canvas, or reduced or enlarged as you wish for finer or coarser canvases.

Right, details of needlepoint wood grain from color picture 23

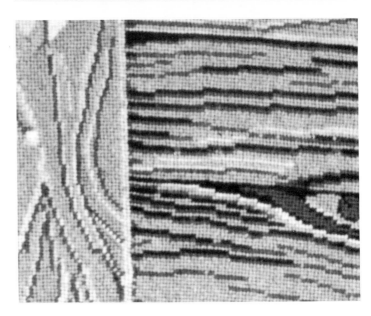

Left, malachite rug. Photostat to about three by five feet. For a square pillow, blow up the top two thirds of the drawing about fifteen inches wide.

Below, malachite slab. This can be used any size. The original sketch was drawn for a pillow fifteen inches in diameter.

there will be no background to fill in later. I was lucky with the choice of backing fabric for the pillow too. Instead of the usual velvet, I happened to find a new kind of crushed velvet that looks as if it had been folded and then steamed. The grain in the fabric is reminiscent of malachite and the color is a true, clear, bright malachite green.

Even though malachite is easy to draw, for something as large as a three-by-five-foot rug it can be a good idea to have the tracing on page 104 blown up by photostat instead of redrawing it freehand. This is only because it can be confusing for some people to try to draw something very much over-scale over a large area. If you really don't trust yourself, a square section of the rug drawing can be blown up for a pillow. And, something I haven't had time to do yet, a tracing right from the printed page could be done in petit point. That would make a facsimile only about double the size of the original little malachite box, which would be getting very close to the scale of real malachite.

The malachite pillow

8 Leopards and Tigers and Other Trophies

Doing fool-the-eye animal skins in needlepoint is an art, but you can do it successfully if you study the real skins. Most of the commercial animal-skin patterns you see are drawn without consideration for the variations in the spots or stripes of real pelts. There is no animal in existence that has the same pattern all over, no tiger with stripes all the same width, no leopard with spots all the same size. And there is an order to the markings of animals, in a pattern that radiates from the backbone somewhat like a Rorschach inkblot.

Leopard Impostor

Lacking a leopard to look at, you can reproduce a piece large enough for a pillow (color picture 26) with the drawing on page 109, for it has a proud forbear, a section right out of the middle of the hide, the best part, which I traced directly from a leopard-skin coat. When I had transferred the spots to canvas, I looked again at the skin and realized that a leopard is not just beige with black spots. There are maybe eight or nine shades of gold and beige and black-brown. A darkening at the center line indicates the backbone. For this pillow I managed with five shades plus black for the spots.

After I had finished stitching a small section, I decided it would be dull business to have only leopard skin over the whole pillow and thought it would be fun to hang something like a medal on it. It took a while to find an object elegant enough to live with leopard skin, but in a design book I found a drawing of this medieval brooch. Fortunately, I had started on double canvas. I traced the brooch

---

Leopard skin, opposite. Photostat to thirteen inches long for life-size leopard skin for the oblong pillow in color picture 26 which was done on No. 12/24 canvas. I used gold and biege Paternayan wool colors 433, 445, 453, 455 and 110 (brown-black). Most people like leopard spots approximately life size, but nevertheless you could make a very effective modern rug by blowing up this tracing so that the largest spots are anywhere from six to twelve inches across. Or, traced off just this size from the printed page, a portion of the pattern would be good for slippers (page 79). Reduced somewhat, you could use it to make something small such as an eyeglass case in petit point.

and the ribbon it hangs on onto tracing paper and traced them into the upper righthand corner of the canvas. Then I stitched them in petit point before I did the leopard skin around them. The stones in the brooch I did last, as I was not sure what colors would stand out well until the setting was done.

The offbeat possibilities for accessories such as this for animal-skin designs are limitless. Because most pillows are used upright leaning against the back of a chair or sofa, a jewel or medallion hanging over the edge like the brooch makes sense. Or something else entirely, perhaps a petit-point butterfly, could appear to be clinging to it vertically. If the needlepoint is to lie flat, on a chair seat or footstool, you might consider a shell, or a peacock feather, or a tropical bug lying on the skin. The trompe-l'oeil effect is more telling if you take into account gravity and whether the final needlepoint will be used vertically or horizontally.

The brooch was an afterthought. It is easier to decide on your decoration at the beginning. Tape the tracing of the jewel or whatever where you want it on the tracing of the animal skin. Then trace everything off onto canvas, bringing the lines of the spots or stripes up to the edge of the accessory. Remember that you must use double canvas, and I suggest that you do the petit-point decoration first, the skin in gros point afterwards. However, if you are uncertain about your decoration, wait a while and if you decide against it you can always stitch the animal spots or stripes over that space instead.

I had this "leopard imposter" pillow backed with brown velvet; color picture 26 shows it with a pillow covered with the real thing. Color picture 25 shows both pillows with a third leopard motif that is something else again, my favorite, a leopard cub.

Leopard Cub

When I saw the leopard cub (color picture 27) in a magazine, I just knew it would be fun to do in needlepoint. Quite frankly, I am hooked on animals and this one seemed to me special. The shape of the cub is a design in itself. The lights and darks and the mottling of his fur are challenging to puzzle out, the pattern is distinctive. The way I did him is "realism" in needlepoint, and an especially careful tracing is shown in picture 27a to show how to work him. But even so, no two people will do him quite the same way. I have seen three or four versions

Brooch from the leopard-skin pillow in color picture 26, actual size.

Leopard skin. Actual size detail on No. 12/24 canvas.

of the cub worked by different people and each time he turns out differently. He is always a leopard cub, but the expressions vary. When one of my friends worked him, he came out a jovial little stuffed toy. I know he will fascinate anyone who likes animals but that each person will see him in quite a different way. What happens is that you put something of yourself into the design and it looks like your work and no one else's. One of the first things to remember in choosing an animal as a subject for needlepoint is that it won't be and doesn't have to be rigidly reproduced or copied to preserve the quality in the original that you like.

The second consideration is that an animal subject has to be small enough in scale to become a pillow. If this had been a full-grown leopard curled up and about to lunge, I would have hesitated — or made a rug.

The third point is where such a pictorial subject will end up. I knew precisely where the leopard cub would live. I had already worked the fake leopard-skin pillow and if the cub were successful, he would live with that, right in my living room where I could see him.

To begin this project, I had the magazine color photograph statted up. It was hard to determine what life-size might mean in a newborn cub, but he ended up of a size to fit into a fourteen-inch circle. The photostat reduced the colors to grays — a value of blue comes out exactly like the same value of brown — and this tends to mute details. To bring back definition between colors and areas, I took a fine black marker, the only truly opaque black that will hold up on the surface of a stat, and outlined the color areas and the spots right on the photostat. These lines became the tracing lines, and this would be the process if you were reproducing some color picture of your own. To do the cub, the best thing is to rephotostat the diagram in the facing color picture 27a; have it blown up to about fourteen inches over all as I did, or any size you want. Your new stat may be a little weak and need some darkening of tracing lines before you use it for retracing onto canvas.

As you can see from the finished pillow, this animal was small and it was fat, and his stance was a big bluff, trying to look terribly tough and not managing it at all. He is a live thing and full of delicate details. Detail was very important to my way of seeing him, so I worked him all in petit point against a background of gros point. Modeling was important, too, and was suggested by the original photo-

Tiger's head. Photostat to twelve inches wide over all for the petit-point tiger (done on single canvas) in color picture 28. When you trace onto canvas, it will help to draw the whiskers in a different color to separate them from the rest of the design.

114

graph. The surfaces that are round and retreating from you, like the area under the stomach, darken as they disappear because they are in shadow. The face, too, is darker on the side away from you. Faithful shading from light to dark gives the whole cub realistic roundness. Even more explicit is the way the pattern of spots behaves as they retreat over the roundness of the back, melding closer together as they go over the backbone.

If you look at the tracing on your canvas as a mass of spots, you will be hard put to figure out where to start. It is far better to plot out specific sections and finish them completely one at a time. My own idiosyncracy is to set an animal's expression first, doing one eye and then the other eye, the mouth and nose, an ear, and so on. This still left me with a mass of spots all around, but the face was building up bit by bit. The same principle applies to the rest of the animal. Plan him in areas: work the paw up to the wrist, then move up to the elbow, then extend to the rest of the limb. You can see next perhaps that the stomach forms a triangle. Do this little pouch next. This method works much better than working by colors, trying to put in all the spots one by one before the colors around them, for instance. This is a dull prospect and makes it hard to see how to do the shading. Change wool colors as often as you need to and give yourself the fun of actually seeing the baby leopard grow as you go along.

You can inject any amount of subtlety depending on your patience and dexterity. You could use a larger stitch than I did and the cub would turn out quite differently and charming in its own way. The simpler your method of stitching and shading, the more naive the result will be, which could be just what you want. I worked this cub in Bon Pasteur yarns which offered some twelve to fourteen leopard colors plus black and white. It could be greatly simplified by using five or six colors of Paternayan yarns. If you decide on a larger stitch, you will probably use fewer shades.

I also worked the background in Bon Pasteur yarns. This was a strange range of colors that go from deep, very brown blue to beige. I started in the foreground with the darkest shades and laid them in, in stripes that are not straight but slanting, so that it is difficult to see where one color stops and another begins. These shaded striations give an almost surrealistic effect of space in the background that is heightened by the almost black shadow underneath the leopard.

You need not be intimidated by the idea of shadows. They are very logical but

23

do not have to be drawn exactly. You have a shadow in position here, but if you want one in some other design, remember that shadows only more or less evoke the shape of the object. They are on the dark side of the object and slope away from the imaginary source of light. If you test how shadows work with a lamp and an object, you will see if you move the lamp about that you can change the shape of the shadow at will and can therefore just draw a shadow that fits well with your overall composition provided that it is properly located on the side away from the source of light.

I thought the earthy, natural colors of the background went well with my cub, and the fact that he blends into it emphasizes that he is really delicate and not very scary. But he has definite outlines and lights and darks. The same animal would be sharp and crisp against any strong, solid background. He would be sensational against brilliant red. (Just picture a leopard coat lined in red satin!)

To further convey the realistic quality of my leopard cub, I chose a piece of real leopard skin for the backing of the pillow.

Tiger's Head

A safari to a record store can yield many trophies for needlepoint designs. The tiger's head in color picture 28 came straight from the jacket of an album called *Never Tease Tigers*. Record albums are today the most graphic of graphic arts and the work that goes into their design often makes them ideal to be reused for other designs. It's a happy accident, too, that record jackets are composed in squares that are already the right size and shape for a pillow.

The photograph on this jacket is detailed and clear. I traced the important features and the main areas of color directly from the album onto tracing paper, then transferred them to canvas, without photostating anything. The drawing on page 113, blown up to twelve inches wide, will give you exactly the simplified tracing I made.

I found I could duplicate the colors in as many colors of Paternayan yarn, though I took the liberty of crisping them up. A real tiger is not as orange as most people think of a tiger as being and the oranges were paler on the album than you see them here.

The tiger is all in petit point. Once again I felt compelled to start with the eyes first, in emerald green, and the mouth, in red, which were to be the strongest colors. Whenever you are doing an animal in needlepoint, whatever expression it is going to have will be in the eyes and mouth. You will probably be most interested, as I am, in giving him this identification in the beginning when you are fired with enthusiasm for the new project and when you are likely to be working at your best, too. Once I had the tiger's eyes in place and the mouth and teeth set, I went into the oranges around them and did the nose. Most of his face was done before I went into the back.

Every needlepoint project poses a new set of challenges. In this case, it was the background that disturbed me most. As I became involved, the tiger got so detailed, with whiskers and hair in his ears, that the idea of a solid background was unthinkable. A friend showed me a wonderful piece of *strié* velvet that looked like blades of grass. I dug out every shade of Paternayan wool in green and ended up doing all the background in petit point too, working random stripes of grassiness one and two stitches wide. It did end up looking like grass with the tiger alive in it. Of course the green *strié* velvet was used to back the pillow.

Mini Tiger

The mini tiger in color picture 30 is quite the opposite of the first one. By shape, by stance, by coloring, he is every inch as much a tiger as the other, but this tiger has been reduced to very simple, stylized lines without much detail or shading. He was done as a pincushion, eight inches long, in three or four colors of silk yarn. There is no modeling on him whatsoever.

The original was a small tiger in a magazine ad which I had blown up. He is small in scale but mighty in effect. Working a normal fourteen stitches to the inch, I could have built him up into a substantial bolster for a sofa (and so could you) or upholstery for a fireplace bench, where he would look very much at home.

I used whatever silk I had enough of, and, even in petit point, with so few colors there were few changes of yarn while I worked this piece. Although I would not necessarily start with the face in so stylized a tiger, I am sure I did anyway. Even so, he looks rather insipid, probably because I was more interested in the body and legs and the twitch in his tail. When I had determined just how he would look, it was important to decide how thick a platform it would take to hold him up.

Since I had left-over silk going begging in my supply, I decided to make the backing of the pincushion in silk needlepoint too, and to try a new binding stitch developed by Hope Hanley (see page 187). With her binding, or edging, stitch, you can join a piece of needlepoint to a needlepoint backing of the same size. I did the backing in flamestitch (color picture 19), joined the two pieces, and stuffed the pin cushion myself with lamb's wool.

Mini tiger. The petit-point original in color picture 30 is eight inches long, but it could be blown up much larger for a bold stylized design.

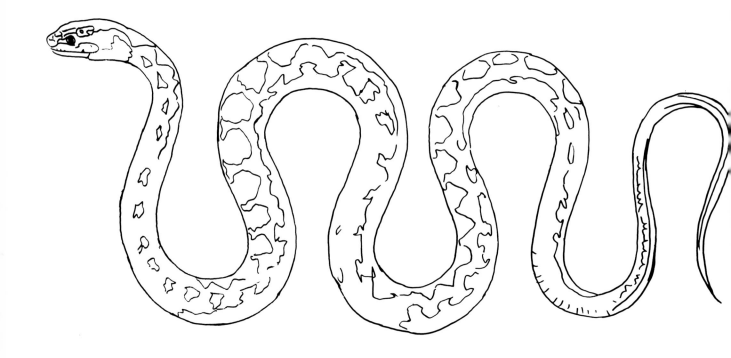

Above, "Don't Tread on Me." Photostat to sixteen inches wide for the snake in color picture 32 worked on No. 12/24 canvas.

Opposite, zebra skin. This is a section of a real zebra skin which will be life size blown up to eighteen inches high for a good-size pillow. The natural colors are off-white and a soft blackish brown rather than the stark black and white of most fake zebra patterns. Taken right from the printed page, these stripes in miniature could be used for small objects such as slippers (page 79), a handbag or glasses case. If you want more light and less dark, switch the placement of colors, making the narrow stripes dark and the wide ones light. The design will be good even if it isn't true to life.

"Don't Tread on Me"

Realistic as the snake in color picture 32 appears to be, I actually took liberties with it. You will never see a real snake coiled like this with his head in profile instead of flat. But this is the way most people picture snakes, and so did the artist of the engraving I took this one from. Just because the outline is completely stylized, I decided to treat the snake as naturalistically as possible, shading the scales in petit point and making him very three-dimensional. In this case I did not have a real snake skin to follow, but the engraving was detailed. Silk yarn brought extraordinary life to the eye. There may be only a dozen stitches of the silk altogether, but the gloss of the silk does make the eye stand out.

In the shading of the scales, I planned that the snake should be moving toward light so that the lighter parts of the scales would be in front, the darker parts toward the back. I used a full range of salt-and-pepper colors to work them. When the snake was finished, I made him look even more real by giving him a shadow of a very dark shade of yellow. The brilliant yellow background sets him off so you cannot miss him. People may think twice before sitting down next to a coiled snake, but they'll never forget your needlepoint.

9 Variations on Themes from Nature

You don't have to look far for sources of nature subjects — books, there are innumerable books on every possible kind of flora and fauna. But as it happens the six subjects in this group came from more offbeat sources.

No needlepoint book would be complete without at least one flower. I feel flowers have been overdone and have stitched very few myself. But if you have a favorite flower, there is no reason why you cannot find it represented in some original way. The anemone is my favorite and on the pillow in color picture 29 I treated it life size as an object, rather than doing a conventional floral arrangement. The detailed drawing was cribbed from an announcement of a vernissage by a British painter of flowers. I had it blown up to the size of a real anemone, traced it onto the canvas, and referred to the original for the detailing. The whole pillow was done in petit point and it is eighteen inches high.

The announcement was black-and-white, but anyone who admires anemones as I do knows the foliage is blue-green and the flowers are white or rich shades of either purple or red. I chose red and it was a case of getting a good range of tones all in one family of red. I found five Paternayan reds which, with white and black for the center, made the flower come alive. The big hollow stem is blue-green, almost slate. Against a yellow green background, the stem and all the leaves stand out; the greens actually fight each other. For the backing, the red of the anemone was picked up again in linen velvet.

Two of my favorite subjects appear on the pillow on page 124, mushrooms and a salamander, discovered on two different old book plates in a New York print shop. The mushrooms are the amanita variety which have bright red caps and white stems. The golden salamander is black with brilliant yellow stripes. Both seem at home on an earthy brown background where you would expect to find mushrooms and salamanders. The boxing of the pillow is a strip of gros point like the background, joined to the face of the pillow with red-velvet piping the color of the mushroom caps.

The fierce owl in color picture 31 is shown almost actual size, a detail from a reproduction of a painting which I did because I was so taken with the texture and markings of the owl's feathers. Six and a half inches square and all done in silk petit point on gauze, 30 stitches to the inch, it was a long time in the stitching. Obviously I referred a great deal to the original in working this owl. To show off the detail, it is stretched flat and framed rather than made into a soft pillow.

Mushrooms and salamander

28

The big bold horned owl on page 132 is altogether different though just as fierce. It was taken from a reproduction, probably of an early American print, that I found in one of those big cut-rate bookshops that always have some kind of pictures for sale. He was done on request and hangs over the fireplace of a country house. On a canvas twenty-four by eighteen inches, the owl is about life size; he would not have so much authority any smaller. Once I got that piercing stare in the eyes, in petit point, the expression was set. The rest of the bird was done in realistic colors, but since the print was simplified and stylized, it was easy to do in a big coarse stitch. The background is bright, bright red.

The two shells in color picture 33 I traced from a printed fabric by Quaintance. Neither one is of a shape to stand alone on a square pillow. I arrived at this surrealistic composition by moving the tracings around within the square and tracing them off again together. Then I added very heavy shadows and the trompe-l'oeil shadow box around them. The shells are stitched in their natural colors, a purple pectin and a beige-and-brown Venus's comb. The background is done in two shades of green, with the paler green on the floor of the shadow box. There is a brief explanation of how to cast shadows and make a shadow box around a composition if you don't think you can draw them yourself. To make your own shell composition, try changing the tracings on pages 130 and 131 to various sizes and rearranging them some entirely different way.

The autumn leaves in color picture 34 should be as irresistible to needlepointers as real piles of leaves are to children. The design came about in the most direct possible way. I just collected a bunch of good autumn leaves, arranged them overlapping inside the pillow outline, and traced them off life size. Not a leaf is repeated in the all-over pattern and I used every autumn color I could think of — greens, browns, reds, deep purple, orange, almost everything except blue. (This is a marvelous way to use up leftover yarns.) In tracing the leaves, only the outlines are important. You can draw the few necessary veins in the leaves freehand. The design was worked on No. 14 single canvas, which is too coarse to do much detail, but, as in a painting, the leaves look very real from a distance while the stitching makes them look quite different close to.

The backing of this pillow is inky green velvet, so as not to fight but rather frame the little pile of fallen leaves.

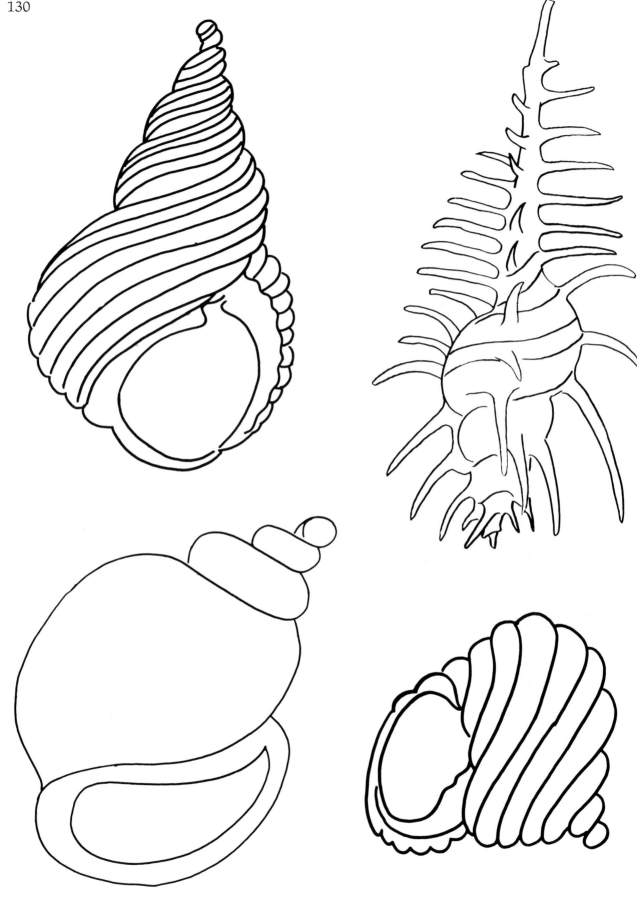

Shells to use in your own compositions

10 Designs from Challenging Sources

Once you start looking for sources for needlepoint designs, you begin to see them everywhere. From rare engravings you must seek out to the daily paper where you might not think of looking, there is graphic material just waiting to be seen with a needlepointer's eye. I am caught especially by European picture postcards, which are often so well printed that the postcard, after you have made a photostat and tracing of the subject, becomes a perfect portable reference for details when you start to work.

I am not suggesting that beginners nor those who do not like working much detail will often choose the type of subject I have in this chapter, nor if they do, will work them in the same way. But once you become interested in very detailed needlepoint, it makes more sense to meet the challenge of a really good graphic source than to put that kind of work into something ordinary. Most of the following pieces were worked on No. 14/28 double canvas.

The figure on the pillow in color picture 35 is the Pompeiian bronze called "Satyr with Wineskin" and I found it on a picture postcard. To model it, I used the same range of French wools that are in the background of the leopard-cub pillow (page 114) because they reminded me of the colors of bronze when it ages — from dark brown-blue to beige. All the dark parts of the figure were worked in blue instead of black, and instead of white I used the palest tint of blue in the highlights. I knew exactly where this pillow would go, on a red sofa. Brilliant red is the color of the background, which also throws the figure into strong relief.

The figure and head of Michelangelo's David in color picture 37 were blown up from two postcards. The sculpture itself is one of the most magnificent works in existence and I did not consider doing the whole figure in detailed needlepoint. Instead, I chose to do a careful rendering of the head and only a symbolic rendering of the figure in the background. I was fascinated by the prospect of doing sculpture entirely in black, greys, and white, and this range of neutrals is well represented in both Paternayan and Bon Pasteur yarns. The game you must play is entirely one of shading and modeling rather than of putting down colors. I worked the head first, in petit point, in five or six greys and black, and then did the figure in just two tones, black and a grey, only picking out the highlights. The background is blue and green, but with a difference. To silhouette David's head, I used solid blue. Behind the figure is a related green, and the rest of the

Horned-owl wall hanging

background mixes a strand of blue with a strand of green. Green velvet proved an appropriate backing for this pillow.

From another postcard came Verocchio's cupid, a fountain in Florence, on the pillow on page 135. It was done in a range of blues instead of greys, from white to blue-black, the idea being that fountains are wet and water usually reflects blue. For the background I chose another blue, out of the range of those in the statue.

In color picture 38 is the Triton fountain in the Piazza Barbarini in Rome, and for this I again used black, greys, and white. It is a complicated subject, also taken from a postcard, and a test of how much detail I was capable of achieving in petit point. The background is a sunny green and the fringe trim added a quality of Renaissance richness to the finished pillow.

The two little dolphins, on page 136, with their tails curled against a shell identify a fountain in the Piazza Colonna in Rome. I never came across a postcard of this, so I used my Minox camera and had the picture enlarged to the size I wanted to work. The range of greys and browns I used left much to be desired in subtlety, so the fountain ended up looking stylized. The subject could have taken any bright color as background, but since I made the pillow for friends with a Siamese-pink living room, that is the color I chose.

It is amazing how many prints of engravings from old books declare themselves as subjects for needlepoint. Because they are usually not in color, you might not think of this at first, but many old prints are beautifully designed and drawn and are very good sources indeed.

The formal design in color picture 4 is one of the few subjects with flowers that I have ever fancied. It was taken from an old engraving at the library of a pair of crossed ram's horns with "flowers" that are an unusual combination of plant materials: anemones, wheat, oak leaves, a pomegranate. The needlepoint was made for the back of a very stately carved cathedral chair that required a design that took itself seriously. But the motif was fun to do. I invented my own more or less realistic coloring. The ram's horns are grey-beiges, entwined with pink ribbon, the flowers and leaves are worked in natural colors, all against a brilliant red background.

The Roman helmet in color picture 36 came from another engraving in the library print room, a Piranese. I made the helmet gold with red feathers. The shading was blocked out just as it appeared in the print and I stitched each element

Dolphin fountain in the Piazza Colonna in Rome

Poseidon, god of the sea, from a Greek coin

individually — the sphynx, the centaur wrestling with the lion, the feathers one at a time, then the visor. The background is green-gold and double shadows were added to lift the helmet right off the pillow.

Poseidon, god of the sea, riding a dolphin, on page 137, is a design on an ancient Greek coin which I found illustrated in a book on Magna Graecia in Southern Italy. I had it statted so the whole coin would be the size of a pillow. I was intrigued by its irregular shape and learned that when the Greeks coined gold 3,000 years ago, they simply put a die on top of a block of gold, hammered down on the die, and the excess gold around the edge made the coin lopsided. The shading around the edge of the needlepoint imitates the irregular rim of the coin and the same crooked outline was kept when the pillow was mounted. I also used very orange-gold colors, the color of old Greek coins.

The Medici coat of arms in color picture 16 was taken from a handsome rendering on the cover of an Italian travel brochure. There was enough variety in the symbol to occupy me for quite a time, doing the crown to imitate beaten gold and precious stones, the carving of the crest painted and gilded, and the five balls of the crest shadowed so they seem raised right off the surface. The design was so vividly colored that it had to go on a very muted pale-beige background. I added in needlepoint lettering an old saying that is a favorite of mine and seemed appropriate: "God created the world, but He sculptured Italy."

Tom Lea's illustration for his book *The Brave Bulls* turned into the needlepoint exercise in silhouette in color picture 14. All the detail in the original (and there was a lot of it) was put on first in black, then everything else including the background was filled in in red. The whole canvas is just these two colors, yet there seems to be much more going on. Although the figure is done in petit point and the background in gros point, you are not aware of this because the same red moves through both areas of stitching.

The source for the pillow in color picture 15 was a United Nations Christmas card, designed and donated to UNICEF by the artist Hans Erni. It looks like more work in needlepoint than it actually was. The simple white lines were done first, defining all the areas of color which were then very easy to fill in. Line was everything in this design, so the original hardly needed to be simplified at all to be transferred to canvas.

The original of the second statue of David, in the Academy of Florence, opposite, was an illustration in the book-review section of the Sunday *New York*

Statue of David on silk gauze, actual size, and detail to the right

Times. Like the painting of the boy with the mobile (page 99), this is the only piece of its kind I will ever attempt, though for different reasons. The photograph shows the needlepoint actual size, two by three and a quarter inches, mounted on a leather bookmark, and the object was to see just how small needlepoint could be done. Now I know, and I am not going to go through it again.

On very expensive pieces of imported needlepoint one used to buy with the design already worked, there were often flowery French ladies whose hands and faces were worked in a stitch so fine you needed a magnifying glass to appreciate them. I learned that these were done on silk gauze which was then appliquéd on the canvas. About one yard of this gauze is manufactured each year, and I was lucky enough to be given four square inches. The only yarn fine enough to work on the gauze is one-ply silk yarn, and that is a thread that makes the eye of the finest needle look like the Lincoln Tunnel. Every stitch meant something, the light had to be excellent, and I should have used a magnifying glass because even the tiny holes in the gauze were distracting and made it hard to see the needlepoint in progress as an over-all design.

A more sensible way to do a piece of this sort is to work on No. 18 or 20 single canvas. Miniature needlepoint does make beautiful bookmarks. When it is stitched, trim the canvas, leaving about one fourth of an inch margin all around. Turn this under and glue the needlepoint, with a white glue, directly onto a strip of leather, then glue a piece of felt to the back of the leather.

11 *Coloring Your Own*

The designs in the preceding Chapter 10 are of a kind not recommended for beginners, but they do bring up something a novice needlepointer should tackle early. This is making up your own color schemes for designs derived from sources that you find only in black and white. Many of the most fascinating sources listed on page 187 are printed entirely in black-and-white line, for instance. So now what do you do?

The best thing to do is to rely on the wools themselves. The colors are so tempting they will get you started of their own accord. The sections on color on pages 63-69 will give you some theoretical guidance. And consider that, even with a color original for your design, the fact is that you always make many color decisions of your own, perhaps without quite realizing it. An exact match can never be available for every color in the original. It is rare that you do not choose your own background color. And if you are a beginner trying to keep things simple, you essentially choose your own colors by limiting the number of them.

When you have no color original, the process may actually be simpler than when you do. You make up your color scheme according to the wools you can get, without interference from colors in an original that can't be matched. You are free to use deliberately only colors appropriate for the room where the needle-point will be used. You can even choose a favorite color scheme first and then plot a design for the colors instead of the other way around.

Finally, remember in using black-and-white drawings to start designs (this is just as true of sources in color) that just because some drawings look quite realistic does not mean that you have to fill them in with realistically shaded colors. That is one way to do it. Another is to use exactly the same outline for a flat pattern of contrasting colors that, in an entirely different way, will be just as effective and a lot safer for an inexperienced needlepointer. So don't be misled into thinking that line drawings don't supply you with enough guidance for your designs. On the contrary, they may be the best sources to use when you have special color requirements of your own or when you don't want to be pushed into anything too complicated.

Since acrylic paints are so easy to handle, make a color sketch of your design with them first (page 63); make an extra tracing of the design and fill in the areas with the basic colors you want. Now choose your wool colors, and gradations of the colors in which you want shading, if any. The success of the color scheme

144

really depends on this choice of the actual wools together, and it will depart considerably from your color sketch, just as it would from a color original. Then, after you have traced all the outlines of the design onto the canvas (page 64), fill in the acrylic colors in each area on the canvas, too, if you want. But as I have said before, painting in the colors could be not only unnecessary but even confusing. Your color sketch may be guidance enough for placing the wool colors.

When you start to stitch, completely finish one small area at a time so you can see how your colors and shapes are working. Do all of one petal of a tulip, the adjoining petal, the whole flower. Or perhaps you are doing fool-the-eye marble. Put in the several shades of marble veins and some background next to them to test the effect. If some color doesn't seem to be right, go buy another one that will do better. You are morally in the clear because you have already saved yourself untold sums of money by doing this yourself. You have not launched into anything really very difficult, though you should, for designs of any complexity, continue to finish each little area before doing the next or you could get confused. Don't, for instance, fill in all the dark sections of all the leaves of a plant, and then go back and fill in all the next sections of lighter green. Stick to one leaf at a time so it grows as a unit and it really will come out looking like a leaf. And work things "in front" before you work shapes "behind" them — as a flower before the leaf behind it, the shadow behind the leaf before the background the shadow falls on. This is not only to keep your colors in control, but also to control the outlines of the shapes of the design.

The line drawings in this chapter are ready to be used with colors of your own devising. The original dimensions were from fourteen to eighteen inches wide and the drawings can be photostated back up to whatever size you need for pillows or chair seats. You will be able to trace directly from the photostat to the canvas. No. 12 or 14 canvas will be better than No. 10 which usually makes designs hard to work because it is too coarse. There is no need to use realistic colors any more than realistic shading unless you want to. Mushrooms can be red, white, and blue if you choose. There is very little detail and no shading in the drawings, so they will serve beginners well treated as colorful patterns. But some of them could also be worked on double canvas with petit point, modeling, and fool-the-eye shadows for a very different effect.

29

30

33

34

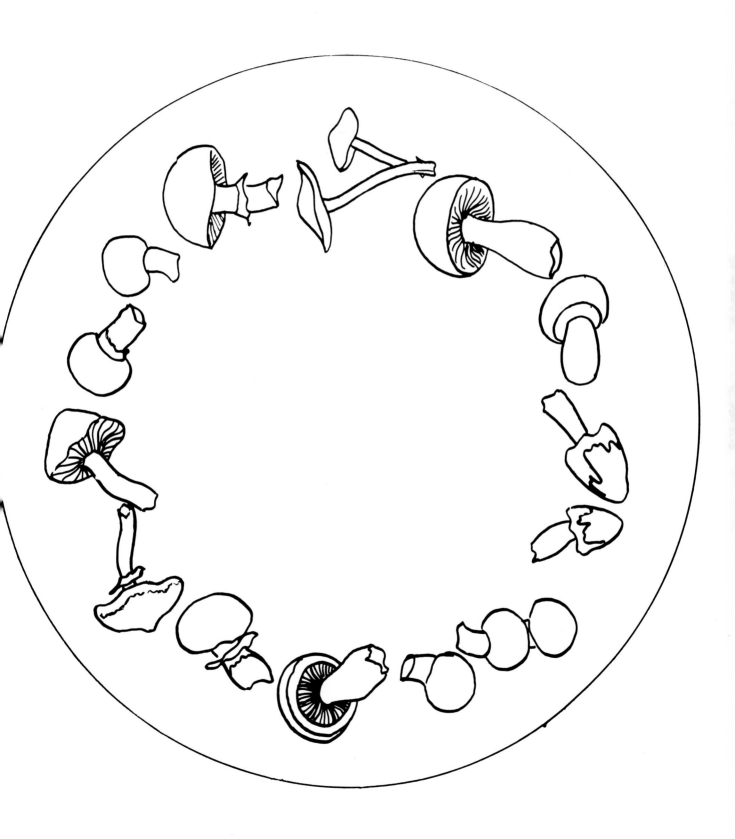

Satiro con Lotpe - Pompei

36

37

38

12 Needlepoint Rugs

To me, any needlepoint rug that is less than ninety per cent pattern is dull to do. That much pattern would be overwhelming on a rug six feet by eight feet or eight feet by ten feet, so I usually make a rug only three feet by five feet and the impact would be hard to beat with anything of comparable size. In fact, I have never been able to live with my needlepoint rugs after I have finished them because they all turn out to be powerful things and my home does not need any more pattern than it has already. But that is my own idiosyncrasy. Choose a pattern that is right for your room. Then if you make it three feet by five feet it will be of a convenient size to be seen from beginning to end on the floor, which will give it real importance in the room. It can be used by a bed or a sofa and will be large enough to hold its own as an accent rug on a bare floor or even on a larger rug or carpet that has little or no pattern.

The drama of needlepoint rugs is only the first thing to recommend them. They are also one of the hardest-wearing floor coverings in the world. People who make their guests walk around rather than on their needlepoint rugs have all the wrong idea. The rugs wear well, clean beautifully, and are mothproof because the rug yarns are mothproofed. Moreover, nowadays the dyes are fast.

No. 10 canvas, forty inches wide, is a good size to tackle and easy to hold in your lap. You may think at first that that sounds like a lot of stitching and wonder about using Quick Point canvas (page 24). This canvas will speed things up, but the rug might just as well be hooked. You could make handsome rugs with it using big bold geometrics such as some of the repeat patterns in the samplers in color pictures 19 and 21 or the caning pattern in color picture 20. However, I think you might be cheating yourself by taking the easy way out. There are very good manufactured rugs of this sort already on the market, so why bother? You will find, moreover, that counting stitches for repeat patterns over a large area is just too much regimentation and not enough fun.

If you want an easy, bold, modern design, it would be far better to use No. 10 canvas and to take something like the fool-the-eye patterns in Chapter 7, have them blown way up, and carpet your floor in oversize leopard or zebra. Or, on page 104 is the tracing for my favorite oversize fool-the-eye pattern, the malachite rug in color picture 24. A marbleized pattern, which you would do with a natural-size vein, is not terribly complicated and the veins of the marble can run through the entire area of the rug. This means you will not have to put in time on yards

Paisley rug, color picture 39, three feet by five feet

and yards of solid-color background without a break. You may have guessed that I am anti-empty-background. Putting in acres of wool in a single color is just plain boring and you can't afford to get bored on a project like a rug. On pages 166, 167, and 174 are the tracing and color suggestions for a rug like a floor inlaid with several colors of marble. This really is quite sensational and not difficult to do.

The three finished rugs shown in this book have one design element in common: movement. The malachite pattern could have gone on and on, and so could the paisley pattern in color picture 39 and the butterflies in color picture 40. The paisley and the butterflies were adapted from huge, bold fabric designs already big enough for a rug, so the scale did not have to be changed and the tracings were made directly from the fabrics. You can duplicate them by having the tracings on pages 163 and 165 blown back up to size, and of course any design you choose can be enlarged to hold its own on a rug.

The paisley rug pattern did take some adjusting, however. It did not have to be rearranged for a three-by-five-foot size, but the tracing eliminated a lot of squiggly lines of detail that could not have been transferred successfully to rug canvas. The fabric, a dress fabric, was printed with a border running down one side. By running the same border motif around the four sides of the rug, I found I could confine the pattern and give some order to it. The colors seemed to make this necessary. A nice ladylike paisley in blue and white might not have needed the frame of a border, but the almost vulgar orange and pink and purple and green of this did. I had to adjust again when I chose the wool colors. I kept the original colors but added muted versions of them, and these tied all the bright colors down. To bright parrot green I added sections of a very muddy green. To complement brassy yellow, I added a tarnished gold. In making such decisions about color, I cannot emphasize too much how important it is to lay out your wools in a good light and consider in advance the effect of the colors on each other. Then once you have a pile of wool colors that pleases your eye, you can start. There are about twice as many colors in my paisley rug as there were in the original printed fabric.

The butterfly pattern was on a velvet upholstery fabric. You can imagine the luster the colors had. But more important than the richness of color printed on velvet was the use of white and a dark brown-black in the design. These, especially the white, play off against the bright colors and give them still more life. Every

needlepoint rug, no matter how colorful, should have some white in it and probably some dark that is almost black. Flecks and streaks of white can be more piercing than shocking pink in needlepoint. So the butterflies were ready to be made into a rug just as they were, and they seemed so alive that I did not confine them with a border but just let them hover on and on.

On the following pages are tracings of a number of rug designs that can be blown up by photostat to three feet wide or larger. They are more conventional designs than those of my own rugs though they do not need to be done in conventional colors. Colors are not indicated, as these depend so much on the room in which a rug is to be used. I have included floral patterns which many people like for needlepoint rugs. I have often been asked to design them though I have not stitched one myself. Remember that photostats large enough for transferring a rug pattern to canvas usually have to be made in sections and taped together, as few photostat shops have equipment for huge blowups. If you want to make a rug over three feet wide, you will also have to stitch it in at least two sections unless you use the unwieldly sixty-inch width of canvas. How rugs done in sections are seamed is explained on page 182. I don't suggest your blocking your own rugs, though you will get an idea of how this is done in the next chapter. It's not easy and just to begin with you aren't likely to have a great sheet of plywood sitting around for the privilege of serving as your rug block.

The inlaid-marble rug opposite is my great favorite. It was done in three colors of marble — black, white, and terra cotta — but the terra-cotta sections could have been another color: green, blue, golden, whatever you want though it must be strong.

On page 100 is a sketch of marble veining for grey-white marble; blown up to eighteen inches high, it will give you a workable scale for naturalistic veining and the *negative* of the photostat will give you a rendering of black marble or dark marble such as the terra cotta. Notice that the veining all drifts in one direction. This is important, because you must keep the veins going roughly in the same direction in each section of the marble rug and then work the veining in the adjoining section of the same color in an *opposite* direction. This shift in the direction of the veins is what sets the sections off from each other at the edges where they meet. Don't stitch a dividing line between the sections; this would completely spoil the effect of the trompe-l'oeil inlay. Four tones is enough for each

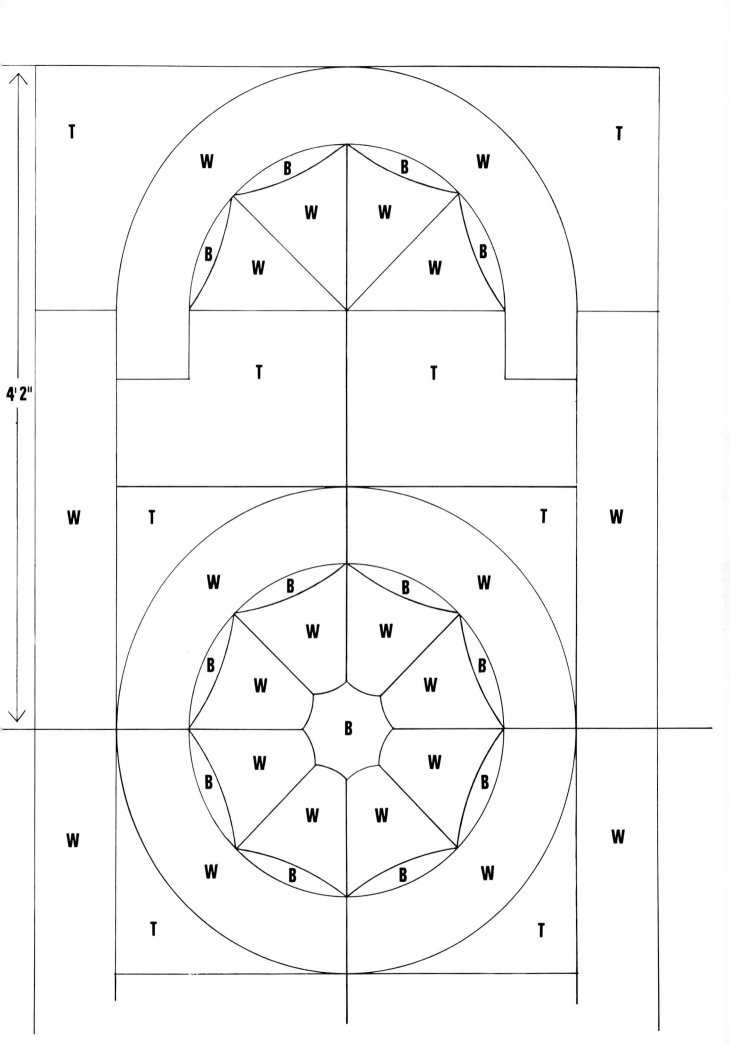

Under-sea rug or piano bench

Opposite, acanthus rug border

Round and oval center wreaths
for ribbons-and-flowers rug

Ribbons-and-flowers rug

marble: B (black) has fine white veins, two tones of dark-grey "clouds" (one grey may be enough in the small black sections of this rug), and black for the background; W (white) has black or dark-grey veins, two tones of light-grey clouds, and white for the background; T (terra cotta) has black or very dark-grey veins and three tones of terra cotta, the two for the clouds lighter than the background.

You need to photostat only one half of the rug, from the top of the semicircle to the horizontal center-line of the full circle; you just repeat the identical pattern turned the other way for the other end of the rug. The original rug was four feet wide and eight feet, four inches long, but this is obviously something you can do any size you want. The center section alone makes a good small rug and on a fine canvas it would make a splendid pillow.

The under-sea design on page 168 was originally made to upholster a piano bench, but it would work well as a rug, possibly with a narrow border added to frame it. The one suggestion to make about color is that the motifs should stand out boldly from the background.

On page 169 is the starter sketch for a repeat acanthus motif to use as a border for rugs. It shows the corner leaf, to be repeated at all four corners, and the motif to be repeated as often as you need it along the sides. The drawing is very simple, with guidelines to use for as stylized or elaborate modeling as you want; work this out completely on one leaf to use as a guide to doing the others. The most successful use I have made of this border was in very bold form, about twelve inches wide. For the center of the rug, rather than another design, use any of the bold geometric repeat patterns in the samplers in color pictures 19 or 21, with a strip of solid color between the acanthus border and the patterned center to set it off.

The ribbons-and-flowers rug on pages 172-173 is not the conventional flower rug, in the sense at least that I was able to use all kinds of garden flowers rather than the eternal cabbage roses that used to infest this kind of design. If you use a seed catalog to look up natural colors for the flowers, you could end up with a blaze of color that will be great fun to work. The design comes in four parts of which you use three: The two halves garlanded with ribbons can be laid out opposite each other to form a square. To fill the center, you would then use the round wreath on page 170. This is the way the rug was done originally. It was five and a half feet square, the center wreath was thirty-four inches across, and the rug was

stitched on two pieces of canvas with half of the wreath on each. For an oblong rug, the two ribboned halves would be laid out further apart, with more space between the ends of the ribbons, and you would use the oval wreath on page 171 in the middle. Both wreaths, of course, would make nice small rugs alone, possibly with flowers in the center (there are some possible flower motifs in Chapter 11), and the round wreath would make a good pillow on No. 12/24 canvas.

The two floral runners on page 178 were the result of a special request, rugs to go in an L-shaped hallway leading to a bedroom decorated with floral patterns. The rugs were to go together but not to match. The designs are each twenty-four inches wide over all, on an unbordered plain background not much wider. The flowers are wildly oversize and very effective. With only a little adjusting at the ends, finishing a stem or adding a flower, these designs could be converted into a continuous border that could be used in any smaller scale, even very small for a petit-point border on a floral pillow. In rug form, these designs were stitched quite realistically, with shading and modeling, despite their size, but they could have been done as a flat pattern with bold and unlikely modern colors.

Floral runners

13 *The Finishing Touches*

Finishing a piece of needlepoint — making it into the final pillow, seat cushion, glasses case, or whatever — is something you may or may not want to do and on the whole it may prove a false economy to try. However, you should know something about it so that you can ask for what you want from the professionals who do it for you. You would be ill advised to mount a rug yourself, but you should know both how you want it seamed and how lined. Something the size of a pillow you might block yourself with more loving care than some upholsterers would do, but you would have to be as expert as he to mount it properly. Smaller items such as glasses cases, coasters, or even a tote bag you might indeed finish entirely yourself, and for such things I recommend highly the book *New Methods in Needlepoint* by Hope Hanley (page 183) who has developed useful techniques for making many needlepoint items. It was her binding stitch that I used to finish the mini-tiger pincushion in color picture 30.

Blocking and Mounting

I feel that you should go through the process of blocking a piece of needlepoint just so that you know what it is all about. But I also feel that when you put a great deal of time and effort into a piece of needlepoint it is worthwhile to have a professional upholsterer make up the pillow or otherwise mount the needlepoint for you.

However, anybody who makes cushions will block needlepoint for you; this is part of his responsibility. Any place where you buy needlepoint supplies has people on tap to send you to, but because you are then relying on a specialist to get this information, the prices for making up your needlepoint may be discouraging. It is worthwhile seeking out your own craftsmen instead. You can pay as much as $75 to have a pair of slippers made up if you go through the needlepoint shop. I sent mine to a shoemaker in Italy who charged $7.50 to make up the most beautiful pair of slippers; it made no difference to him whether he used my needlepoint or his leather. Upholsterers are really the same. To the average good upholsterer, what you have made is just another upholstery fabric, and he charges accordingly.

A small pillow should cost about $10 to $15 to be blocked and made up by your own upholsterer. If you did your own design, you cannot have spent more than $5 to $10 for the canvas and wool. In other words, you could expect the finished pillow to cost a maximum of $20 to $25. It could have cost you $125 had you bought a prepared design and had the pillow made up through the needlepoint shop.

If you plan to block your own canvas, before you even begin your needlework, measure the fresh taped-edge piece of canvas. You will need the exact record of these dimensions when you go about blocking the finished piece.

You need a surface to pin the finished canvas to. I use an old drawing board of inch-thick pine. You can use anything like this that is thick enough not to warp. A piece of plywood is good – it will not warp at all – provided you have room to store it. A sheet of brown wrapping paper taped over the board will keep the surface clean. On this piece of paper, draw the outline of your canvas according to the original dimensions before you started to work on it. When you have finished a piece of needlepoint, the shape of the canvas bears little resemblance to the square or rectangle you began with, being crumpled around the edge and pulled out of line where it has been worked.

Now examine the condition of the edge of the finished canvas. The masking tape may be frayed and broken. When you lift away a bit of the tape, you may see that it is going to pull off some threads of the canvas. Perhaps there is not much blank canvas left around the edge because the design got bigger than you first planned, leaving you with a precarious-looking border of canvas to work with when you pull and haul in the blocking.

I have not actually had much trouble with fraying at the edge of the canvas in blocking, because I use a staple gun for the pinning process that is described below, and I use untold quantities of staples which hold several threads of canvas in place at once. However, if you don't want to invest in a staple gun, or think the canvas really looks unsafe (it will get worse when you wet it), the completely secure thing to do is to gently peel off all the masking tape, turn under a narrow border of the canvas all the way around, and stitch it down with a sewing machine. (You may ask why not do this before you begin to stitch in the first place? Don't, for the turned-under raw edge of the canvas will catch and snag the yarn the whole time you are working on the needlepoint. If you want to sew the edge of a canvas before you stitch it, fold cotton binding tape over it and stitch that down. This is some trouble, but it is very neat.)

Take the canvas to the sink and lay it on the drainboard, right side down. Wet a clean sponge and with it pat the back side of the needlepoint. By the time you have sponged it enough, you should be able to wring a few drops of water from it, but you don't want it gushing water, so don't put it under the faucet. At this point, do not be shocked if the needlepoint is like wet felt. It literally hangs in your fingers and has the consistency of putty. This is not the point at which you cut your throat. You have not made a mistake. All you have done is to dissolve the sizing in the canvas and there is no more stiffness in it.

Now place the damp, limp canvas right side down on the wrapping paper-covered board. Use tacks or push pins, anything that is nonrusting, to secure the canvas to the board. Regular thumbtacks and staples will rust and bleed down into the canvas, so be sure you use steel thumbtacks or staples. Of course, if you have a wide unworked margin of canvas around the needlepoint, this will not make too much difference, but it is best to be aware of the possibility.

First, stretch the damp canvas to the four corners of the outline on the wrapping paper. (If you turned under the edge of the canvas, you must reduce the outline accordingly.) Start pinning at one corner and pin all four corners of the canvas to the matching points on the paper. This is easy. Pull the middle of one side to the corresponding line on the paper and pin or tack it, then pin all along that side, placing the pins half an inch apart. Now pin the edge on the opposite side of the canvas, then a third side. Now you must confront the fourth side. This is hard. Do not be surprised if you have to recruit another person to help pull that fourth side and line it up with the brown-paper pattern. Do not be afraid, either, of tearing the fabric; needlepoint is one of the strongest materials in the world. When it comes to needlepoint rugs, I know that as many as two or three men will be engaged to pull that fourth side of the rug into place on a stretching board.

Next, you must let the canvas dry. It can take several days. Do not put it near a radiator or fireplace to accelerate the process. On the other hand, in a steam-heated apartment in winter a canvas might dry overnight. You know it is dry when the canvas is suddenly stiff as a board again. Take out all the tacks, turn it over, and you will be amazed how well your needlepoint looks. Because you have blocked it face down on a flat surface, the stitches, loose and tight, will have evened up. It must now be steamed to fluff up the yarn. Place it face up on your ironing board, hold a steam iron over it, but do not let the iron press down on nor even touch the needlepoint.

You may have to block the piece more than once. If, after you take it off the ironing board, it seems to have a tendency to go back out of shape, it *must* be blocked again. You may rest assured the second and third blockings are much easier than the first. Do not take any chances. If the piece is not absolutely in line, it will eventually crawl back to its lopside shape after it has been made up into a pillow. The experience of blocking is worthwhile at least once, just so that you know what it entails and can appreciate a good job of blocking.

Seaming Rugs

Rugs worked in pieces can be seamed after blocking in several ways. Traditionally, the method of seaming a rug down the middle is to leave unfinished the last few rows of stitches along the edges that will meet. Then when the two pieces are complete except for these stitches, they are overlapped so that the missing spaces of the design correspond. The last rows of stitching are done through both layers simultaneously. This works beautifully because you can stitch over any number of layers of canvas and never know from the top how many are underneath. The surface stitch is the same size as all the others. This is a miserable job to do, however.

Recently, when I have had rugs assembled by the upholsterer, I completed all the design on both pieces. There were a few inches of selvage which we then folded under. The two lengths of rug were lined up stitch for stitch with a basting thread woven in and out through the two pieces of canvas. Fold one side of the rug over the other, and stitch the seam on the sewing machine along the basting line and as close to the needlepoint stitches as possible. Finish the way you would any seam by folding back the canvas edges and overcasting them. This is the least bulky method. It works like a charm.

A third method which I do not recommend is to finish the canvases and turn under several rows of stitching when joining the two pieces. This makes a bulky seam and invites disaster underfoot.

Rugs are usually lined. I cannot say whether this is advisable or not. It is much more luxurious to have a rug lined and most people do. A lined rug may wear better than an unlined one. I do know that if a rug is not lined, it is less attractive to moths. But the advantages of lining a needlepoint rug and also interlining it with felt are that it will be less likely to "walk" on the floor and will have more body and stiffness.

Shopping Information

The following shops sell blank canvas by the yard and the Paternayan yarn that I have used for most of the needlepoint in this book. They will fill orders by mail. The supply of catalogs, brochures, and samples varies from shop to shop, and it is best to inquire which of these is available (and for what service charge) before placing your order. To match yarn you have previously bought, send your own sample to the shop, specify the yarn color by number if you know what it is, or do both. Shipping charges will probably be somewhat less if you order from the shop nearest you.

The Yarn Depot
545 Sutter Street
San Francisco, California 94102

The Needlecraft Shop
13561 Ventura Boulevard
Sherman Oaks, California 91403

Lucy Cooper Hill
1126 Kane Concourse
Bay Harbor Islands
Miami Beach, Florida 33154

Needlepoint, Inc.
2401 Magazine Street
New Orleans, Louisiana 70130

Four Wives
43 Main Street
Cold Spring Harbor, New York 11724

The Elegant Needle
5430 MacArthur Boulevard NW
Washington, D.C. 20016

Selma's Art Needlework
1645 Second Avenue
New York, New York 10028

The Jeweled Needle
920 Nicollet Mall
Minneapolis, Minnesota 55402

Virginia Maxwell
Custom Needlework Studio
3404 Kirby Drive
Houston, Texas 77006

The shop listed below will fill mail orders for blank canvas and a different and excellent needlepoint yarn which is dyed in a number of colors that are not available in Paternayan yarn. Only here was I able to find the particular range of blues and greens I needed to stitch the malachite pattern for the rug and pillow shown on the frontispiece and in color picture 24. The shop can also provide you, on special order, with canvas for a pillow or rug with the malachite pattern already transferred to it and the wool needed to work it. For other colors in this yarn, and for more of the shop's prepared designs, inquire before ordering what samples and brochures are currently available.

Nantucket Needleworks
11 South Water Street
Nantucket, Massachusetts 02554

The shop listed next sells the imported French Bon Pasteur yarn and blank canvas by mail order. Because of the wide range of tones in Bon Pasteur colors (page 26), you should inquire before ordering about available samples. As was explained earlier, I recommend this yarn for projects that require very subtle shading and modeling. This company also sells Paternayan yarn on order.

C. R. Meissner Company
22 East 29th Street
New York, New York 10016

Depending on where you live, you may or may not have easy access to photostating shops, or may have trouble getting very large stats for projects such as rugs. (You can, however, stat such designs by sections; see page 61.) If this is really a problem for you, the best thing to do is to look up, at the public library, in the Yellow Pages for the nearest large city in your area, the firms listed under "Photo Copying." Inquire by letter whether orders can be filled by mail and at what rates, explaining also the size of your original and the size of the stat that you want. There are hundreds of thousands of photo-copying shops across the country and their operations vary widely; in a major city you should be able to find at least one that can accommodate you. Be sure to specify that you want a photostat, as the same shops may do other, unnecessarily expensive types of photo copying.

Studio Magic Markers are available all over the country, but perhaps there is no art-supply store near where you live. In that event, write to . . .

Customer Service Department
Magic Marker Corporation
84-00 73rd Avenue
Glendale, New York 11227

. . . and be sure to specify that you are looking for the completely waterproof versions of Magic Marker products.

Books and Other Reference Sources

The following books are some of my favorite sources for illustrations from which to make needlepoint designs. The list will give you an idea of the types of books to look for.

The Concise Handbook of Roses by Kiaer & Heintz, Dutton.

The Elements of Design by Donald M. Anderson (paperback), Holt, Rinehart & Winston.

Field Guide to the Birds by Roger Tory Peterson, Houghton Mifflin.

The Flag Book of the United States, by Whitney Smith, William Morrow.

Handbook of Ornament by Franz Sales Meyer (paperback), Dover.*

Handbook of Plant and Floral Ornament from Early Herbals by Richard G. Hatton (paperback), Dover.

Monograms and Ciphers by A. A. Turbayne (paperback), Dover.

New Methods in Needlepoint by Hope Hanley, Scribner. (An invaluable book for techniques of finishing and mounting your own needlepoint projects rather than having them done professionally.)

The Shell: Five Hundred Million Years of Inspired Design by Hugh & Marguerite Stix, Abrams.

The Styles of Ornament by Alexander Spelz (paperback), Dover.

The World in Your Garden, National Geographic Society.

The World of Roses by Bertram Park, Dutton.

In addition, be on the lookout for European magazines such as *Connaissance des Arts* and *L'Oeil;* for books, many of them juveniles, published by Golden Press, on animals, birds, insects, fish, flowers, etc.; and the better American art magazines.

*For a catalogue of many other Dover books on crafts and design, write Dept. DA, Dover Publications, Inc., 180 Varick Street, New York, N. Y. 10014, and write to the same address to purchase Dover books listed here.

Index

About the Author...

LOUIS J. GARTNER, JR., has been an editor at *House & Garden* for many years, as Creative Crafts Editor and as Special Projects and Garden Editor. He initiated in the magazine a highly successful series of articles on a wide variety of crafts and found that needlepoint drew exceptional response from readers. He is also a professional designer and partner in a shop called simply "Needlepoint" in Palm Beach, Florida. He originally chose to concentrate on needlepoint for his own amusement, because it is so versatile, beautiful to look at, and more portable and convenient to do than any of the many crafts he has worked with.